Survival of the Inner Man

Survival of the Inner Man

Queen Kirkwood-Hatchett

Scripture quotations from the King James Version of the Bible unless otherwise stated.

ISBN-13: 9780578174068 (Queen Kirkwood-Hatchett)
ISBN-10: 0578174065

Published by Queen Kirkwood-Hatchett
Printed by CreateSpace. An Amazon.com Company.

Contact the publisher for copies and other written publications at:
hatchettqueen@yahoo.com

Cover design by LaQuilia Graham
Cover Image by Canva

Table of Contents

Dedication

This book is dedicated to the survivors of childhood sexual abuse and to those who have not yet healed.

Introduction

❦

WHENEVER I DRIVE OR WALK by a playground, park, or school yard and look over at the little children playing, I wonder just which one or how many of the girls and boys are experiencing the horror and terror that I did when I was their age. I wonder how many will return home from school and meet a relative or friend of the family at the door, whose sole intent is to wait for the opportunity to molest them. I wonder how many fear and regret the fall of the night because they know what awaits them after dark. I wonder how many have already mastered the skill of hiding the pain of what is happening behind those closed doors at home, and I wonder just how many of them want to tell but don't know if they should for fear of the consequences. I was one of those little children many years ago.

My life was a state of absolute chaos and disarrangement after the effects of sexual abuse, rape, incest, and molestation I had experienced early on in my life began to surface. I spent over thirty years of my adolescence and youth trying to pick up and put back together the shattered pieces from by broken childhood. Confusion about my purpose and destiny; fear; pain; torment from the sexual abuse; and recurring dreams from a past relationship of almost twenty years kept my life in an epic struggle for survival.

This autobiography will explain how I overcame the dramatic and traumatic effects of childhood sexual abuse. The material is clinical, psychological, and spiritual. Males and females of all racial, economic, religious, and social classes will learn that they, too, can overcome the trauma from childhood sexual abuse.

CHAPTER 1

The Beginning of the Trauma

❧

MY LIFE WAS AN ABSOLUTE wreck by the time I reached age eighteen. My inner man was warped. My spirit was completely broken. Psychologically, I was out of it. I was normally functioning on the surface, but underneath the surface, my soul was ripped apart like a lion rips his prey. A chain of events occurred in my early childhood that later threw my life into complete and total disarrangement. My inner man could not handle the subjection to such trauma year after year, so, inwardly, I broke, experiencing too much, too soon, and too often.

Listed below are some of the horrible events that began a serrated journey of disorder, emotional chaos, and sexual and emotional disarrangement in my life:

- A close family member sexually abused me when I was five years of age up until I was about nine. The abuse could have started earlier than five years, but I can only remember as far back as five.
- A total stranger fondled me when I was seven years of age.
- A man who was well into his eighties fondled me when I was about nine years of age. He was husband to one of the church mothers and was on his sick bed when it occurred.
- A schoolmate's brother raped me when I was thirteen years of age.
- A total stranger raped me when I was fifteen years of age, which was the most traumatic experience. It happened at a building about two houses down the street from where we lived. Although

I was with a responsible relative, it was a place from which my mom had warned us to stay away.

I was standing outside the building when suddenly a man came behind me, grabbed me by the neck, pulled me into a station wagon and raped me. When it was over, I stumbled out of the station wagon with my clothes ruffled. I was frightened to the point of hysteria. My mom came to me with a switch in her hand and proceeded to whip me after she found out that I was there. I was crying hysterically, frightened to death, and trying to get away from my mom and the perpetrator all at the same time.

After we had settled at home, I told my mom what had happened. There was no police report filed. And before long, talk of the incident subsided and disappeared like a vapor. Many years later, when I was an adult, my mom related to me that the reason they did not proceed with charges against the perpetrator was that the police officer warned my mom that if we went to court, they would only try to destroy my character; that is a common thing even now. Most women do not come forward because of the embarrassment and because most defense attorneys blame the victim for the incident.

❀ At about age seventeen, a man that I had known since I was a little girl raped me.

CHAPTER 2

The In-Between Years

❦

THE HORRIFYING EVENTS ABOVE INJURED me, set me off emotionally, tore apart my inner man, and brought on the confusion and chaos in my life that lasted for many years.

I tried to escape the pain and fear caused by these unnerving events by suppressing them. I attempted to go on with my life as though none of them happened at all. The defense mechanism that I used was similar to that which I used when my mom prepared to whip us when we were younger. We were beat with long, hard switches and extension cords for our misbehavior. Whippings were very traumatic for me. I recall times when my mother stripped me down to my underwear and whipped me. On at least one occasion, my mother tied one of my brothers to the bed and beat him. That scene plays over in my head from time to time.

There was always a lecture before the whipping. Fear gripped my heart with immeasurable intensity during those times. I created in my mind a *secret tunnel* to which I always escaped in between the lecture and the whipping. I gradually dismissed every part of my body into the secret tunnel, piece by piece, until it was safe inside the tunnel. That was the way in which I dealt with the pain. In reality, there was no escape, just as there was no escape from the pain and torment of the sexual abuse. I learned later that I experienced dissociation. As described by the [1]Mayo Clinic, de-personalisation/de-realization happens when an individual experiences a "disconnection and lack of continuity between thoughts, memories, surroundings, actions and identity disorder." Disconnect happened with me when I dismissed myself from my surroundings and the actions and into the tunnel. I will talk more about dissociation later.

There was more unhappiness in my life than happiness. We never attended parties of any kind, and we only fellowshipped with people of the church. We missed out on many things in which children typically participated in school. I was never allowed to attend a game, a prom, or any other school activity. It seemed to me that I lived in total seclusion and isolation from the world. Holidays were not holidays because the congregation in which my mom was involved did not participate in pagan holidays. Friends were not allowed to come over and play with us, and we were never allowed to spend the night in anyone's home, which was a good thing considering all the times I was molested.

I recall running away from home beginning at around age twelve. I felt I had no identity and no sense of belonging to anything or anyone. I began experimenting with drugs when I was a teenager. I was never a drug addict, though the potential was certainly present. I even attempted to join a friend in prostitution when I was a teenager, but I lacked the nerve and courage and could never build myself up enough to do it.

The abuse came to an end after about age eighteen because I understood that I could say "no" and I learned to fight back. However, at that point, I had a torn spirit, a confused mind, a distorted perception of sexuality, and my body was thrown completely off-balance.

The following twenty-one years of my life I carried memories of the abuse. I felt that pieces of my body were scattered here and there and that the perpetrators lugged a part of me around with them all of the time. Those thoughts generated a sentiment of a lack of order in my life. Even as an adult, before God delivered me from the pain and healed me, I always needed to have someone's approval on every decision I made. I felt utterly incapable of making good, right, and sound choices on my own. I felt the need for the opinion of other people in making the least important decisions that a person my age should have been autonomous enough to make on her own.

SUMMARY

I suppose my mom raised us the best she knew and was probably a bit overly-protective. Even with my mother's seclusion and restrictions, I know for sure that three of the five of us were sexually abused, including at least one male.

CHAPTER 3

The Dark Years/The Lost Girl

❧

AFTER SURVIVING THOSE DARK YEARS of sexual abuse, I understood the reason my life was in such disorder, and why I made such horrible mistakes and bad choices during my adolescence and young adult years.

Before understanding the meaning of life and my purpose for existing, it seemed as though my life were merely hanging in animation, dangling between heaven and earth. My teenage years were the darkest years of my entire life. I had a very low self-perception and was unsure about surviving. I always chose the lower class guys to date and the most unsuccessful friends with which to hang out. After becoming an adult, this was even more evident. Always feeling worthless and unimportant, I could never see myself in any light other than a complete failure. The security of feeling loved, wanted, or appreciated had no place in my life. I always wanted to feel a sense of belonging to something or someone, but the trauma and pain almost shattered my dream of ever becoming anything worthwhile.

I gave my life to the Lord and became a Christian at age eighteen. I did not understand the real meaning of Christianity, redemption, regeneration, and deliverance, and this lack of understanding made me feel that I had to revert to my old ways. Before long, I gave up on Christianity and returned to my old ways. And that was a dreadful mistake.

A few months after I reverted to my old ways, I met the man who later became the father of two of my children. I became pregnant with our first child two years after we met, at which time I was nineteen, and he told me he was twenty-nine. Just as I predicted, he abandoned my child and me. The situation was very favorable for my low self-perception and added more pain to my wounded soul. I tried to hold on to the relationship, but how do you hold on to someone who is not even there? The dream of ever being married to him and raising our child together in love was only a dream to me because I thought that such a good thing could not happen for me.

I moved out of the state to be with a man that I had known while pregnant with my first child. He had been in prison most of the time that I had known him. The relationship was very toxic and unhealthy. He pulled a shotgun on me several times and threatened to kill me, accusing me of being unfaithful. Subjecting myself, unaware, to more abuse, I found myself falling deeper and deeper into a well of despair.

Living in the house in which I moved with him was two of his brothers, his oldest brother's girlfriend, his father, and his aunt. His oldest brother was a drug abuser, and his youngest brother was a drug dealer. His father and his aunt were both alcoholics. I left Michigan after staying only thirty days because his aunt threatened to kill me for reasons still unknown to me. I moved to Chicago with my sister, feeling lost in what I called the "sea of no hope." I tried to pull myself up and do better, but life became even more confusing.

I was unemployed with no means of financial support for my child, only a high school education and pain from the incident in Michigan. I consistently searched for employment but began to feel that it was hopeless. Being twenty-two years of age at the time but never having a full-time job, for the first time in my life, a severe spirit of depression engulfed me, and this is what happened:

I stood gazing out of the window of the seventh-floor high-rise building in which we lived, and something very strange happened to me. I was holding my daughter around her waist as her legs dangled out of the window. A very compelling voice spoke to me and told me to let go of her so that she would fall to her death and then all of my problems would be over. It was such an active voice! It tried to convince me that all of my problems would be over if I got rid of her. It further said to me that I had only to take my arm from around her waist, and that would be the end of all of my problems. Immediately following that voice, a very soft, sweet, and reticent voice whispered to me not to let go of my daughter. It said very distinctly to me that I loved her, and if I let go of her, I would regret it. The other voice came hastily behind that soft voice again and told me to let go of her, and that I would easily escape. Well, this battle over my daughter's life and death went on for a few minutes. Finally, the voice prevailed that was so soft, sweet, and distinct. The other voice sounded so convincing and reasonable that it almost convinced me that letting go of my daughter was the right thing to do. It was as though I were under a spell or in a trance.

I loved my daughter, indeed, and she was surely not the cause of my problems. My problems began long before her birth. The spirit of the Lord convinced me to hold on to my daughter. What was happening to me at the time is that all of my failures and disappointments, as well as my dark past and despairing future, overwhelmed me, and my vision became cloudy. I could see no future, and I felt there was no hope. It seemed to me that my whole world had come to an abrupt end. Not very long after that incident, I was blessed to secure employment in the downtown Chicago Loop.

I wrote this poem for my daughter a few years after the episode in the high-rise building.

My Daughter (Queeda Lynn)

I love you dearly, Queeda Lynn
For you are my only child-
Given to me by God, above
For just a little while.

There is so much in life to see-
So very much to know-
So many roads to travel down-
As you learn and grow.

But I'll be walking by your side-
To help you to contend;
And I'll be there to lend a hand-
Whenever you need a friend.

As long as you are in my care-
I'll help you carry on;
Until you are vigorous and vibrant enough-
To stand and walk alone.

When I see a news flash that a male or female has physically abused or killed their (child)ren, I reflect on my experience in Chicago with my daughter's legs dangling out of the window of that seventh-floor high-rise building. Compassion fills my heart. Harsh words, harsh language, and destructive criticism are very easy to find when the shoe is on the other foot. But harsh words, brutal language, and destructive criticism are as equally hard to find when one has come close to or walked in another's moccasins.

SUMMARY

Filicide is the deliberate act of a parent murdering his or her child according to [1]Wikipedia. The word "filicide" derives from the Latin words fillie, meaning "son," filial, meaning "daughter," and cede meaning to kill or murder. [2]Dr. Phillip Resnick, director of forensic psychiatry at Case Western Reserve University in Cleveland found in a 2005 study that filicide is the third-leading cause of death in American children ages 5 to 14, and that mental illness and depression are factors in the murders. Resnick further asserts that "Historically, one out of 33 homicides is a parent killing a child younger than 18." In the same article, it reports that each year, 250 to 300 children are murdered by their parents. [3]One government statistic indicated that between 2001 and 2010, the official number of child abuse and neglect fatalities was 15,510. This number is staggering and depicts what is going on in American households.

Sometimes I play back the experience in my mind and wonder what would have been the result had I listened to the other voice. My speculation is that I would be spending my life in prison at this very moment. My name would have flashed across most television screens, giving a very gruesome and dramatic account of the incident. People would have wondered why or how I could have committed such an evil and immoral act. Well, now you know! When depression, gloom, doom, despair, and hopelessness set in the spirit, life becomes meaningless and a problem. It is very easy just to end it all. Ending it all means stopping the pain. In my case, and in my mind, ending it all meant getting rid of my child, because, in my mind, she was the problem.

There are essentially four voices that exist on the earth; the voice of God, the voice of the devil, our voice, and the voice of other people. God rescued me by speaking to my spirit and guiding me to safety from the murder of my daughter. The devil's voice was the evil voice, and my voice had no power at the time because I was lost in a cloud of depression. God was merciful and graceful to come along and deliver me from the destruction of my daughter and myself.

CHAPTER 4

Displaced Love

❦

LIFE IN THE CITY WAS very fast and confusing for me. I grew up in a tiny town and was not accustomed to the fast, city life. During the time I lived in Chicago, I became involved in a few relationships that added to my injuries. First, I reunited with a man that I had met some years prior in my small hometown. I did not stay in that relationship very long because he was too strung out on drugs and was never alert long enough to know even what a relationship was.

I reunited with another guy that I had met several years prior while visiting my sister in Chicago. He was handsome, well-mannered, intelligent, and any woman's dream man. I had a suspicion, though, that he had become bisexual. I was incredibly naive about the bisexual lifestyle. I dated him for a few months and broke off the relationship because after leaving work early one morning and going to his hotel room, I found him in bed with another man. Unaware of how to compete with a man for another man, I abandoned the relationship.

Shortly after leaving the relationship with the bisexual guy, I met a pimp. Yes! A real, live pimp! Not a "want to be," but the real deal. He was nothing shy of one of the most handsome men I had met, ever. He was very generous when spending money on me, and treated me better and with more respect than I had ever known. He tried very hard to oblige anything that I asked of him, while consistently complimenting me on my personal appearance, my intelligence, and physical attractiveness. He often told me what a smart girl he thought I was and how he felt that I would be very successful in life.

When I first met him, he told me that he wanted an "innocent girl." I understood his definition of an innocent girl. He wanted a girl who wasn't a prostitute. We often discussed his lifestyle and our future together. He insisted that he could never obtain average employment because of his lack of education and skills, and he knew no trade. He never propositioned me about being a prostitute during the time we dated, which made me feel very special. The feeling, though, was sick and self-deceiving.

I discontinued my relationship with him after one year. The relationship was one of the most unusual in which I was ever involved. Deciding to break away from him was one of the hardest decisions I ever made because he treated me (I thought) with great respect, and he was always exceptionally kind to me. I discontinued the relationship because I could not accept the fact that he would be nothing more than a pimp, and there would always be those other women in our lives.

I became involved with a man who hustled on the streets for a living after ending the relationship with the pimp. I became pregnant, had an abortion and abandoned the relationship because I did not want a hustler for a future husband or father for my child.

A short time after leaving the relationship with the hustler, I stumbled upon a young man whom I dated while living in the south during my teens. Feeling nostalgic, we both thought that since we knew each other from way back, we could have an adamant, trusting, and lasting relationship. We tried to make it last. However, it lasted only weeks. I ended the relationship on account of his environment. He lived in the heart of the ghetto of Chicago, and I could not adjust to those conditions and the pressure that came with them. I became pregnant with him during our short time together, and that pregnancy also ended in an abortion. It felt as if I was on a merry-go-round at that point in my life because things were happening so fast. I went back to work without ever taking a leave of absence or having an examination after the abortion, and became deathly ill. The illness could have been a result of neglect of medical attention after the abortion, a botched procedure, or that I became sexually active again too soon after the abortion. The event below details the nauseating description of what happened that dreadful Saturday morning:

I awakened feeling frail, faint, sick, and the taste of death in my mouth while at the same time, feeling the life in my body slowly slipping away from me. While lying there in bed for a while, I came to realize that I had to fight if I wanted to live. I refused to lie in bed and die but was too weak to walk, so I crawled to the kitchen, crying and praying as I went, knowing that if I had died, hell would have been my home. I was not fit to die, and only the mercy of God was able to sustain me and keep me alive. I do not know why I wanted to try and eat because I certainly was not hungry for food. However, I crawled on the floor and made my way to the kitchen. I gained enough strength, by the grace and mercy of God, to stand on my feet and slowly move around. I gained enough strength to open a can of vegetables. After eating the vegetables, I slowly crawled my way back into the bedroom, praying and crying along the way. After more crying out to God and asking Him to spare my life and believing Him for it, I felt strengthened, and could slowly feel life returning to my body. I knew then, as I know now, that beyond any doubt, prayer and the mercy of God are what allowed me to survive that horrible episode. I never shared with anyone up until this time, what happened that Saturday morning because I was too ashamed to let anyone know what brought about the illness.

I did, indeed, meet some brilliant, wholesome, educated, ordinary guys in Chicago, but feeling unworthy, unable to meet up to their expectations, and undeserving, I stuck with what I felt was my kind. Giving myself to men of low esteem was my comfort zone. What I wanted, I did not feel good enough inside to receive. If God had not come along and rescued me, self-destruction would have been my end, because my low self-perception and the pain and fear kept me paralyzed.

A few months after the abortion, I became exhausted of the city life and nearly overdosed on drugs and came close to having a nervous breakdown. I finally decided to leave the city in the winter of 1979, emotionally exhausted, and spasmodically panting for relief from myself. I left with my mind pivoted on modifying my life. Tired of all the dead-end relationships, tired of the city life, and just plain sick of being tired, I was more than ready for a change.

The portrait that you may have painted of me at this point may suggest to you that I was a street-walker, dirty and tacky, and hung out waiting to pick up guys. But my style was quite the contrary. I was a very hard working girl—not on welfare as some may assume. My dress style was very impeccable and professional. I lived in a relatively decent neighborhood with my sister, and not the "projects" as some may assume. I was reticent, soft-spoken, not at all rowdy, very petite, and knew how to carry myself as a lady. I received many compliments from guys on my feminine posture and physical attractiveness. However, the men who complimented me could not see my inner person. It doesn't matter what other people think of you, or what they see on the surface; it's what you think about yourself, how you feel about yourself, and knowing who you are.

The perception that I had of me was partially due to the psychological pain and injury that resulted from years of physical and sexual abuse. On the outside, it appeared as though my life was exemplary. However, anyone with any psychological or spiritual insight or discernment would have concluded that I had a very microscopic self-perception, which was evident by the type of men with which I involved myself.

Summary

I can now identify abusive men and can also identify women who are needy, thirsty, desperate, and hungry for love, affection, and attention. Some males and females carry some of the same characteristics; have the same needs, and most of them exhibit them in the same manner. Women who harbor low self-perception always settle for men who are below their standards. They always select men who are incapable of meeting their needs. Abusive men prey on such women. The strange thing is that men who choose needy women are also needy, which is why they select women who will take care of them, women from which they can take and never give back, and offer only a small amount of support. Such men are also in need of the affection, love, and attention they never received. They are familiar spirits. They attract each other. When they become a unit, the relationships are rarely successful, and the women end up giving birth to and taking care of children who are born with the same spirits, and it becomes a vicious cycle.

The daughters, unless taught differently from their mothers, will experience the same thing(s) their mothers experienced. The path the girls take may not look similar on the surface, but the cycle will be the same. For example, one of my daughters did not date a pimp or have abortions, but, she, too was in a relationship cycle, attracting the same type of men.The cycle was fast and exhausting, causing her, too, to leave "the rapid city."

CHAPTER 5

Imprint on the Soul (The Story of J)

WHEN I LEFT CHICAGO IN 1979, I did not leave a Christian, but I rededicated my life to Christ soon after returning home. Many changes took place in my life between 1971 (the year that we left my hometown) and 2000. One change merits particular emphasis. From 1971until around 2003, I experienced recurring dreams. I was a Christian in 1979 and did not understand why I was dreaming about someone with whom I was involved many years prior. The dreams came about four or five times a year and were about a guy with which I was involved while living in Missouri. I will refer to him as J. The dreams came to be very disturbing to me after some years. I began keeping a journal after concluding that they were significant. After carefully examining them, I noticed that J and I were never intimate or sexually involved and we always ended up going our separate ways. These components led me to understand that rather than the object of my dreams, J was a symbol. God began revealing to me the meaning of the dreams.

The dreams started after my family left Missouri and moved to Illinois in 1971. J and I broke up, and I felt a void in my heart. The love and compassion that I felt during our relationship kept me subconsciously in search of the same type of relationship. J was never in the forefront of my mind at the time of the dreams, and I did not have an overwhelming desire to be with him after I left Missouri; maybe not consciously.

After some deep soul searching and understanding of J's position in my dreams, I concluded that he left a very deep imprint in my heart at one point during our relationship, and here is the reason:

J lived on the "good side of town." He dressed nicely, was very, very hand-some, intelligent, and in my opinion, well-mannered. He was in the mili-tary at the time. As for me, I lived in the less developed area of town. Our house was a shack. We did not have the luxury of modern facilities such as restrooms inside the house, televisions, and telephones. We were still burn-ing coals and wood and using a potbelly stove. We worked in the cotton fields to have clothes to wear to school. My mom worked extremely hard to take care of us. She was sometimes involved in training school out of town, and I was left to attend to myself and my brother. My wardrobe was near to nothing. My hair appeared unattended most of the time. I was forced to look after my hair all on my own. We did not have access to the luxury of perms and other current hair care products and tools. Many times I went to school feeling awful and sorrowful because I dressed so poorly. Our clothes were always clean, but they were not the best clothes. In spite of all that, J chose me over the other nicely dressed, beautiful girls.

One day in my junior year of high school, J came home on furlough and to the high school. A girl who had a crush on him saw him before I did and began flirting. She became very hostile toward me when I showed up, and she demanded that J chooses between the two of us. J made a choice between the two of us, and he chose me over her, openly, in front of her friends and mine. I knew at that time that I had something special with J and that our relationship was genuine. The affection that he showed to-ward me was beyond my comprehension. There I was, poorly dressed, feeling very insecure, and unattractive. The other girl was neatly dressed and much prettier than me, I thought. No one had ever stood for me the way J did that day. He chose me in spite of how poor I was. From that day forward an imprint of what happened remained in my heart.

Even though the school incident was positive for me, it was also the begin-ning of the recurring dreams. God was beginning to show me why, but a very tragic thing happened before I understood. Instead of remaining observant of what God was revealing to me, I did some research, discov-ered where J lived and took a trip to visit him on impulse. It had been over seventeen years since I saw him. I thought the trip would improve some things. I moved out of my emotions, out of my flesh, and out of my intellect, and ended up with some very devastating results.

I became pregnant while visiting J. It was one of the most devastating and disappointing events that had happened to me in my Christian life, and one of the saddest as well. J and I concluded that we both were living different lives and things had changed so much for the both of us that there was absolutely no way we could be together. The dreams concluded that we would never be together. I should never have taken the trip to visit J, and we should have never been intimate with each other. Just as the Bible says:

> *Can a man take fire in his bosom, and his clothes not be burned? (Proverbs 6:27)*

After I had returned home, I did not know at first that I had become pregnant. J never knew that I became pregnant. I aborted our baby with the deepest regret. There was hardly a way to express my feelings after the abortion. Being pregnant by a man that I had dreamed about for so many years sent me into a state of anxiety. I did not know what to do or with whom to talk. I was ashamed of my actions. Facing the church, friends, or family was more than I thought I could handle. What would be my explanation? I was a Christian. Well, just as the Bible says:

> *"Righteousness exalteth a nation, but sin is a reproach to any people."* *(Proverbs 14:34)*

Pride and fear of having J's child, knowing that we'd never be together was more than I thought I could handle. I became very depressed when I discovered that I was pregnant, and after the abortion, I became very numb. That abortion, I felt, was different from the others. There was an added element. It wasn't *just another aborted child.*

I cried and continuously prayed until I reached a point that I could not cry anymore, but was still in emotional pain from the abortion. I thought that God would never forgive me for having that one selective abortion. With the other abortions, I felt forgiven very quickly and without a struggle. But this time, it was different. I was a Christian, and it was J's child. Once again, I reached a point where I wanted to give up on living a Christian life. I continued to go to church services, and I was serious about the things of God. But I was torn and struggling on the inside.

I was in prayer one night concerning all that had happened, weeping and crying out to God when I felt a strong spirit of forgiveness overshadow me, and I eventually forgave myself. It wasn't that God had not forgiven me; I had not forgiven myself, and the abortion was tormenting me. Instead of living in victory and peace, the tormenting spirits of guilt, unforgiveness, fear and agony nested in my inner man.

As far as the recurring dreams about J, God was speaking to me about my need of healing of some disturbing emotions with which I was wrestling. They were unresolved issues that led back to my need for love during my childhood. I felt a lack of love in my life during my entire childhood. J was the only love I had experienced up to that point.

Before my knowledge of what are recurring dreams, they were appearing to me. After doing some research about dreams and their meaning, I discovered that the authors were exactly right concerning my dreams and visions. According to [1]Dr. Margaret Bowater,

> *"most of our dreams are symbolic pictorial representations of our response to current issues in our lives, produced by the inner self on the "inner screen" of the mind."*

Also, concerning recurring dreams, [2]Dr. Angel Morgan disclosed that:

> *"Often, a very important message for the dreamer that has been ignored will repeat until it's understood or worked through by the dreamer. It's kind of like a dream is saying, "Hey! Remember me? I'm back! When are you going to pay attention to me?" Some anxiety-based dreams will repeat tasks that are unfinished in the dreamer's waking life. These kinds of repetitive dreams tend to repeat until the waking life task at hand is completed."*

[3]Evidence also concludes that "recurring dreams occur during times of stress, and once the problem has been resolved the dreams will cease." To sum it up, recurring dreams sometimes indicate that there is an issue that needs addressing. The implication of my dreams was that I did not feel loved, even as a Christian. Subconsciously, my past relationship with J was what I reflected on when I was in a stressed out situation and needed to feel loved. The essence of my dreams of J was that I longed in my heart for love and affection. I never felt loved when I was a child, never experienced the warm embrace in the arms of a father or mother, never recall my mom or dad hugging me and telling me that they loved me, and I don't remember being hugged or kissed on the cheek or forehead while growing up at home. My grandparents were not affectionate, although our families lived under the same roof many times. My only real experience of feeling love, affection and safety were in the relationship with J.

What God worked in me was the truth that man did not have the absolute love of which I was in need, or for which I was searching. I was utterly destitute and deprived of love, and I was starving from the lack of affection in my life. The love for which I was searching, even as a Christian, was in Jesus Christ. That is a very strange thing, because God is love, and, as a Christian, I had Him living inside of me, yet, feeling deprived of love. God's love is the ultimate love needed to fulfill my life. It was not that God didn't love me, but I didn't feel loved by Him because I never felt loved by anyone else. Through that experience, I learned that we could allow people to cause us to feel unloved by God. To counter that, we must believe John 3:16, 17 and take it at face value.

[16]*For God so loved the world, that he gave his only begotten Son, that whosoever believeth in him should not perish, but have everlasting life.* [17]*For God sent not his Son into the world to condemn the world; but that the world through him might be saved.*

It doesn't mean that we are nothing because people treat us like we are nothing. It doesn't mean that we are not loved by God because we never receive as many gifts and ornaments other people receive when they are cherished, respected, and honored by other people. People will be people, and we cannot compare God to them in any sense of the word.

We feel the way we feel about ourselves sometimes because of the way in which other people treat us. For instance, I never had a birthday party when I was growing up. I had only one birthday party, and it was when I was in my late twenties. Up to that point, my birthday was just another day. It didn't mean that I didn't exist because I never had a birthday party.

I experienced skin hunger during my entire childhood and part of my young adult life. [4]Skin Hunger is "a lack of affection and touch in which individuals have a strong desire to be touched and a high need for love in their lives." I will talk about skin hunger later.

When I grew older and discovered how good it felt to be hugged by someone, I wanted hugs all the time, and I wanted to hug everyone. A hug and a touch have in them a message, no matter what the real intention may be. There are good and bad hugs and touches. The contacts that I received when I was molested and raped were bad and wrong, and they were intended for evil and not good. The hugs and touches that I received from people when I grew older were most of the time sincere, healthy and genuine, and made me feel very special and good inside. What I unearthed about touch and affection during research was that they could play a significant, influential, and decisive role in determining and governing our emotional and psychological survival.

When I was about six years old, I loved to sing a song called, "I Never Knew Love until I Met the Lord." Sometimes the church people gave me money to sing that song for them. I look back on those times now and realize that even in our childhood, when we know nothing of the issues of life, God is ministering to us. When we are totally oblivious to the many things that happen to us, and things that are said to us, God is somewhere behind the scene speaking to us in a voice that we will only understand as we mature. He sets us up for the future. I had no idea that such a song would be the essence of a dire need in my life. However, God knew that later on, and down the road, that song would become the motherboard of my life. It would be the very thing that would bring me up and out of my depression; love was the key to my deliverance. It was the very thing I later realized was missing in my life. I never knew love until I met Jesus. The Lord Jesus Christ ministered His love and grace to me in such a way that now, I can sing that song, as Paul says, with an understanding (1 Corinthians 14:15).

SUMMARY

When I was about nine years old, I dreamed that one of my uncles were shot and killed, and another wounded but survived in that same dream. It was not very long after the dream that both of them, the same ones I saw in the dream, were shot on the same night. One of them died, and the other suffered a gunshot wound but only survived because he ran for his life. Dreams and visions have always been a part of my life. But growing up in church during my early years of Christianity, I heard many preachers discount dreams and visions, claiming that most of them resulted in eating pork. They claimed other ill-suggested beliefs, judgments, and opinions about dreams. However, I knew that there was much validity to my dreams and I came to a conclusion after I had been a Christian for some years that I had the gift of prophetic dreams and visions. I continue to have dreams and visions, and I came to realize that God gifted me with such.

CHAPTER 6

The Beginning of the End

⤳⤳

I MOVED BACK HOME WITH my mom in in November of 1979, and my life took on a new meaning. Giving my life back to Christ put me on a very smooth plane. I felt fresh and hopeful, had a new attitude, and lived in an entirely new environment. The atmosphere was more serene and peaceful. God had restored me and refilled me with His Spirit. I was elated about my new life, and everything was wonderful; however, internally, the wounds from my past lay dormant.

In 1980, I moved out of my mom's house and began my new life with my daughter. But memories of the past began to surface and haunt me after a year or so, and my refusal to communicate with God about them only made things worse. As painful as it was going to be, it was imperative that the issues surfaced. It was years after giving my life to Christ that I mentioned the abuse in my prayers. I had to learn first that I could communicate with God about such things, not understanding or knowing the Word that reads "He came to set the captive free." (Luke 4:18)

The subject of sexual abuse and many other sexually perverted topics were taboo in our church congregation, and from what I learned then and know now, it is still taboo in many religious groups across America. Fornication and adultery are the only two subjects that I have heard many men and women of God speak on or preach about in church congregations across the country. However, in recent years, homosexuality in many groups across America has become a major issue and is being debated in the Christian community and mentioned in pulpits across the country.

I spoke with some women of the church congregation of which I was a member and found that some of them suffered sexual abuse during their childhood. I wanted to understand what had happened to me and thought that maybe there were some answers among my sisters in the church. One close friend disclosed to me that she was abused sexually by her father, who was a preacher. Another friend revealed to me that she was also abused sexually by her father for many years. One female confided in me that the man she was with presently had sexually abused her daughter. A woman that I talked to many times about the way in which she was abused sexually revealed to me that she had survived incest as a child. All of these sexual abuse issues (and others of which I was not aware) were present within a rather small congregation of about two hundred fifty members or less, and none of the issues were addressed, discussed, or even talked about except among each other. Because the problem of sexual abuse did not seem to be a concern in the church, I never even contemplated counseling. I needed to speak to God about my issues. Just as the other women, I concluded that these were issues that I had to deal with outside of assistance from the church.

I began communicating with God about my past, which made my relationship with God even stronger. My communication with God about the situation was not as strong as it should have been as I think about it now. My communication with Him should have been more often and with much more intensity. I was not yet aware of and didn't understand the degree of suffering and the devastating effects of CSA (child sexual abuse). I had no first or second-hand knowledge of how it could generate so much disarrangement and confusion. More importantly, I was totally unaware of the healing process for such a disturbance. I only knew that something was wrong and I needed intervention, deliverance from the pain, and someone with whom to talk.

When I was in my thirties, I made my mom aware of all the times I was sexually abused. She was utterly shocked. She was especially shocked when she learned that a close family member molested me. Some time later, more of my female relatives began unveiling their experiences of sexual abuse and how family members, friends, and strangers molested them. The same men molested some of us. One of my female relatives revealed to me that the pastor of a church molested her. One of my male relatives also told that a female relative molested him. I felt relieved to know that I was not alone.

Secrets in families can sometimes destroy families. Some children are not aware that sexual abuse is wrong, but once adults know there is a perpetrator among them, it is their duty and responsibility to inform and warn other family members of the problem. Keeping the problem a secret empowers the aggressor and allows him/her to abuse perpetually. Even now, some members of our family refuse to acknowledge the reality that these events took place, and they feel that we should leave the matter as is.

The character of men that I chose to marry after I became a Christian gave great insight to my low self-perception. The emotional trauma of the sexual abuse carried over into my adolescence and young adult life which drastically affected my thought process, and as a result, my thought process affected my ability to choose a suitable companion. By the time I was forty-three years of age, I had married three times, and the longest either marriage lasted was two years. All three men were identical in economic, educational, intellectual, and social class. They were all uneducated, had been incarcerated in the past, and were either physically, verbally, or emotionally abusive, or all three.

My first marriage lasted only six months. By that time, I had been a Christian for five years and was devastated that my first marriage failed after leaving a life of sin behind. I filed for a divorce after my then-husband tied me to the bed, raped me, sodomized me, and beat me. I filed charges against him, and he was found guilty on the local level and sentenced to prison. He filed an appeal and sadly, and to my surprise, he won the appeal and was released. During the trial, I learned two things: number one, I was pregnant, and number two, he was a convicted murderer and released from prison not very long before I met and married him.

My second marriage, which had the most devastating impact on my life, was the father of my first child and my last child. Because we already had a child together and had matured since we first met, I was confident that things would work out fine. Not so. The marriage lasted nearly two years, and during that time I became pregnant. My then-husband left me during my first week of pregnancy. When I discovered that I was with child, every mistake that I ever made hit me like a ton of bricks. Despair became my constant companion. Misery was by best friend. Every single morning that I awakened, there was a throbbing pain in my heart. My heart ached from the hurt of knowing that I had been abandoned again by the same man. I didn't realize until my son was born that I had been severely depressed for the majority of my pregnancy.

My failed marriage haunted me during most of my pregnancy. I grieved with what seemed to be unbearable grief from the sadness of the possibility of having to raise another child without him; the same man that abandoned me at nineteen years of age with my first pregnancy. I only felt depression as I saw the real picture. The reality was that I had been left again by the man that I had loved, trusted, and so humbly forgiven for leaving me the first time with our first child. I almost went into a state of paranoia. I felt like I had come to the end of my life. How did I ever end up in such a situation? I wondered what was wrong with me most of the time. How did this happen to me? I pondered these questions nearly every day of my pregnancy. I had reached a point where I honestly did not know what to do from day to day.

One day during the midpoint of my pregnancy, while I was in prayer, God told me that He was going to cause my heart to sing. I loved music and singing. But during the time of my pregnancy, there was hardly a sound of music playing around the house, and I found no song suitable enough to sing. I knew in my spirit that God had spoken to me, and a feeling of confidence that my situation was going to change began to settle into my mind. I did not know how or when things were going to get better, but He had spoken to me, and when He speaks, things happen. He confirmed it to me two more times before it came to pass. My situation did not get better immediately, but things did indeed change. God delivered me from the depression. He also wanted to give me complete and absolute deliverance and inner healing from my painful past. But that happened years later.

One night in the final months of my pregnancy, God showed me a vision. In the vision, I was climbing a very tall and rugged mountain.

Climbing the mountain demanded every bit of toil and effort I could produce. For some obscure reason, fear began to grip my heart with immense intensity. As I looked down, I saw an unfathomable depth. It was such a depth that no human could imagine, and only one's spirit could vision. Neither my eyes had seen, nor had my mind ever imagined such depth. I had a few choices. I could remain in my present position on the mountain in fear of falling, continue climbing that hard and rugged mountain, exerting every ounce of energy I had with every movement of my body, or I could give way to fear and fall an ineffable depth to my death. After realizing my choices, I stood still, and a voice said to me, "If you pray in the Spirit, I will deliver you." I knew that this was the voice of the Lord. I began praying in the Spirit, and instantly I awakened, still praying in the Spirit. The message was very clear and the vision was one of the most vivid I ever had. The message was to pray in the Spirit, and it would bring on my deliverance. There is a difference in praying and praying in the Spirit. The word of God reads in Romans 8:26:

> *"Likewise the spirit helpeth our infirmities: for we know not what we should pray as we ought: but the Spirit itself maketh intercession for us with groanings which cannot be uttered. And he that searcheth the heart knoweth what is the mind of the Spirit, because he maketh intercession for the saints according to the will of God."*

My freedom did not come overnight; it was a process. However, I held on to the vision with all my strength, believing God was surely going to help me to overcome the trauma from my childhood. My belief was that He was not only going to deliver me out of my present dilemma, but that He was going to give me complete deliverance from all of the years of hurt and pain, the haunting past, and from the things that compelled and influenced me to make such awful choices.

I talked with my then-husband about the pregnancy during the second month of our separation but did not hear from him or see him again until our son was four years old. Something remarkable and beautiful started taking place in my life when my son was six weeks old. It began the end of my troubled past and helped to usher in my deliverance. It started one night when I sat with a friend and listened to a message ministered by a very power evangelist. Among other things, the message was one that ministered Jesus' love and compassion toward His people. She ministered about the things that God has prepared for those who love Him. It was a message of hope for me. I had been experiencing abandonment and rejection issues throughout most of my pregnancy, and most of my life in general.

I saw Jesus in a brighter light. He ministered to me the things that eventually brought me up out of the well of emotions that were controlling my life, and that had trapped me for so many years. It was incredible! I found myself forgiving everyone who had ever offended me, beginning with the relative who molested me, to my husband who had abandoned me with the young child that I had at the time. Nothing in the world mattered to me except Jesus and loving everybody, which was the first step to my freedom.

I felt an entirely new sense of life as Jesus began to minister to me who I am in Him. From that day forward, my mind was riveted on walking in who I am in Christ. Instead of looking at myself as abandoned, hopeless, defeated, and rejected, I began to see myself as a winner, an overcomer, and successful. Feelings of low self-perception, along with some other emotions had been dictating to me who I was, what I was qualified for, and what I did and did not deserve. Although this new revelation was like a breath of fresh air, I knew that it was not yet over, and I did not have the complete freedom that I desired. I now needed healing. But I did know that the healing process had already begun.

My third marriage lasted only about thirty days and was one of the most regretful ones. The most hurting thing that I experienced from that marriages is that I put my children through some experiences that may have traumatized them.

It appears that I would have known better than to involve myself with such men. But I was drunk with the wine of hurt, pain, fear, torment, and low self-perception. These emotions had taken control of my life. I was yet learning how to walk in the Spirit. Walking in the Spirit denies the flesh control of the emotions.

This I say then, Walk in the Spirit, and we shall not fulfill the lust of the flesh. (Galatians 5:16)

Emotions will always be a part of our human nature, but they should not control our ability to make wise choices. They are to be checked by the Spirit of God. I had not learned how to walk in the Spirit, and the things that I was experiencing within the Christian lifestyle that I had taken on were totally unfamiliar to me. Hurt and pain that I experienced when I began walking with God were easier to understand and manage. But how could I handle something that I brought over to the Christian life with me, and how was it there? I did not know how and I did not know why. However, years later, I came to understand the scripture that says:

Submit yourselves therefore to God. Resist the devil, and he will flee from you. (James 4:7)

This passage of scripture means to open up to God and become vulnerable to His Word, giving fear, pain, hurt, torment, anxiety, and all other emotions into His hands. He is capable of handling them. It means to obey God and walk in His Word even if we do not understand what is going on, or why. Early on in this chapter, I expressed a dream I had about a mountain. I was trying to carry the burden up the mountain because I had not entirely submitted to God, but God tells us in His Word to speak to the mountain (Matthew 21:21).

SUMMARY

After the marriages, I was nearly over the hardest part of my journey. Getting very near my forties, everything that had happened in the sexual abuse arena, I felt, was over. I was almost safe now, except for having to deal with the fact that I was probably going to have to raise my children alone. My heart bled for my family. I cried many, many nights because of the pain I knew they would suffer as a result of the horrible choices I made. I cried for them because as children, I knew the pain and hurt they would experience later in life because of the absence of their fathers. I prayed for the health and security of their emotions long before they realized there was no father in the home. I experienced much torment, and I had to fight it, always. I never denied the mistakes and the wrong choices, but I knew that I could not live in torment the rest of my life. And at some point, I had to give my children up to God and ask Him to be the Father to them that none of us had.

When I became a Christian, I didn't feel deserving of a Christian man. I never considered that I was good enough for a Christian man because I already had a child before becoming a Christian. I felt defective. I also believed that because my sexuality was in such disarray, I didn't qualify for a Christian husband because they were spotless, decent men. I thought that if a Christian man ever learned that I had been sexually abused or raped, he would abandon me. I assumed that he would believe that I was an awful person. These thoughts were controlling, influencing, dictating, and affecting my decision-making process. Although the feelings were real to me at the time, they were lies and tactics from the enemy to keep me in bondage. They were reasons that I kept marrying men outside of the Christian arena.

CHAPTER 7

In Search of My Father's Love

MY MOM AND DAD WERE married about six years when he decided to leave my mom for another woman. At that time, I was only a few months old. So, he was not present in our home while I was growing up. My mom gave birth to two children from other relationships after my father abandoned the family. She raised five children without support. At one point in the late '60s and early '70s, her income was a mere $175 a month. I take my hat off to her for having the courage to raise us alone. She deserves much praise and applause for her endurance; however, my father's lack of financial and emotional support and the other men's lack of support posed a tremendous strain on the family.

I cried many days and nights for my dad and felt an intense need for him during my teens. I wrote to him often, but he never wrote back. Years later, I discovered that he was illiterate, which partly explains why he never wrote back. It felt good writing to Dad because I could tell him about me and sometimes describe my problems to him. Most of the time, I knew that there would be no response. Nevertheless, I wrote.

I believe that if my father was in the home, there is a strong possibility I would not have been abused sexually or molested and that I would not have chosen the type of men that I did. I would have been able to see just what a real man was. And there's just something special, in my opinion about the presence of the male gender in any place. The very existence of a man carries a distinctive aura of protection, security, and safety.

I never knew what it was like to be loved or shown genuine affection by the male gender, never received hugs, kisses on the cheek, a pat on the back, or compliments of any kind from either parent during my childhood. I believe that is why I felt such a strong attachment to J. He displayed much genuine affection to me, especially with the incident at school. He showed me that there was more to the male gender than what I had experienced, which was only abuse, neglect, abandonment, and rejection. I haven't involved myself in another relationship with a man that was as genuine, affectionate, and compassionate since my relationship with J. At the time, he was the epitome of true love to me. It is no wonder that I continued to see him in my dreams year after year. All of this was wonderful, but even J could not take the place of what I longed for in my heart. I longed for the presence of my father.

There is a possibility that J did not have as much love for me as I felt he did. Maybe it was all an illusion. Maybe J was not giving me as much love as I thought because of my desperate need at the time. I was so empty, so destitute, and so deserted of love and affection that it did not take very much at all for me to feel engulfed in love with anyone who showed me the least affection. If God had not come along and rescued me, I would still be vulnerable and easy prey for any man who would show me the least affection or attention. The type of men with which I became involved proved it.

There were certain things at my immature stage of life that I needed to see, hear, touch, feel, and experience from my dad that could have steered me in a different direction. I needed my dad to be the model and example of a husband. Since I did not have my dad, and after my relationship with J, my perception of a man was the sum of the negative experiences I had with men, and it was dreadfully distorted.

I felt hopeful that my dad and I could make up for lost time and we could have a close relationship as long as he was alive. After all, we had begun communicating via telephone around 1980. I even went to visit him for two weeks when I was twenty-one years of age. Even though he had a new family, I felt very special being in his presence. It was a feeling beyond what I can verbally express. I felt that nothing or no one could harm me because I was with my dad. At twenty-one years of age, it amazes me that I could still feel protected and secure in his presence.

My sister, my oldest brother, my mom, and my oldest daughter traveled to a family reunion. Although we were supposed to have been going to a family reunion, for me, it was "going to see my dad." The meeting was fantastic! Although I was twenty-six years of age at the time, it was positively sensational for me to see my mom and dad communicating. Even though I knew their marriage was over, when I saw them talking together, I smiled euphorically. Dad wholeheartedly apologized for abandoning us, and he explained what happened from his perspective. He acknowledged that he made a foolish mistake by walking out on his family. We all fought vigorously to keep from breaking down in tears. There was no question as to whether or not we forgave dad. Because we loved him, we forgave him as if it never happened.

We did not know at the time that we were beholding our dad alive for the very last time. We drove all the way from Illinois to Mississippi and back on a cracked motor. We did not know when we started out on the trip that the noise we heard all the way there and back came from the crack in the motor. The car completely broke down after we returned to Illinois. God held the motor together for us because He wanted us to see our dad before he died, and only God knew that we would not see Dad alive again.

Dad passed away seven years after the reunion. It broke my heart. My dream shattered of ever getting to know him. Oh, my God! It was over. He was gone forever. The only Dad I ever knew and loved. How could I get Dad back? I couldn't. He was gone from me forever. I looked forward to being a part of his life and he a part of mine. We were at a point where we were communicating on a more regular basis. Then suddenly he was zapped out of my life. I felt robbed, cheated, and that Dad had been taken from me unjustly.

I needed something or someone to fill the void, and only God was capable. I did not know how things would turn out, but Dad was gone, and I needed God to help me through the pain and to fill the void. He did fill the void. He filled it in a way that I never imagined as He took me all the way back to my childhood. He showed me that it was He who was the Father all the time; He was the absent Father. Even after I became an adult and lived alone, He was right there all the time, protecting me like I felt protected in the presence of my father at the family reunion. Who else stood by me during all the times of my distress, loneliness, fear, depression, trials and tests? It was God who was there all the time, being Father. And He was the One who made it possible and fulfilled my dream of spending time with my earthly Dad.

SUMMARY

Living without my father when I was older seemed more devastating than living without him as a child. The chance to be around him and share our lives, I felt, could have brought some healing to my damaged soul. Even though I was an adult at the time of his death, his advice to me about relationships could have possibly saved me some heartache. Having someone in which to confide would have been a plus. I am sure that as my father, he would have been happy to help me in securing a proper relationship with the right person.

Fathers are meant to head the home, to defend the family, to stand at the door of the lives of everyone in the household, and to spiritually, emotionally, and physically shelter them. Without this layer of covering, children are vulnerable, and they become available prey as they would have the appearance of a defenseless family because there is no father present. It is not to say that women are incapable of being strong and emotionally supportive of their children, but that is not the correct design.

I believe that separation or divorce of man and wife is one of the most devastating experiences that can occur in a child's life, and sometimes the most traumatic. Guilt, frustration, confusion, low self-esteem, anger, loss of identity, and a host of other emotions can begin a journey of incalculable trauma in a child's life when parents decide to separate or divorce. In my opinion, no matter how strong, smart, or intelligent a woman is, and regardless of how much money she makes, her strength, wisdom, knowledge or elaborate income will never take a father's place.

As a single mother, I do not believe that women can ever be both mother and father to their children because that is also not the design. I have often wondered how a family can fail when there is a loving and caring father in the home who stands guard at the door of the life of his family.

CHAPTER 8

A Look at Who I Am in Christ

IT WAS A WHILE BEFORE I realized my position in Christ after giving my life to Him in 1979. I had to learn to believe, accept, and act on that position.

> *But ye are a chosen generation, a royal priesthood, a holy nation, a peculiar people, that ye should shew forth the praises of him who hath called you out of darkness into his marvelous light. (I Peter 2:9)*

I was being controlled by pain, fear, and hurt from my past experiences. But when I became new in Christ, I had to undergo a metamorphosis:

> *And be not conformed to this world: but be ye transformed by the renewing of your mind... (Romans 12:2)*

I allowed my emotions to control the area of my life that the spirit was meant to control. My mind had been defining who I was, but the mind that I was allowing to dictate to me was not that of Christ.

> *Let this mind be in you which was also in Christ Jesus. (Philippians 2:5)*

Through His Son, Jesus Christ, God, who is full of mercy, ministered to me just who I am through His Word. God says that I am the King's daughter. An earthly King would never give his daughter away to a man who is not of a particular royal status. The president of the United States would never contemplate giving his daughter away in marriage to a man who is uneducated, financially unstable, one who has a lack of social class and grace, unintelligent or without good standing within our country's social standards. To do so would be degrading not only his daughter but himself also. The men with whom I involved myself were as peasants compared to the King's children.

It was never God's will that I yoked myself with men that abused me so badly. He wanted me to have a man of royalty. Because God loves me so much as His daughter, He did not allow destruction to come to me because I chose to marry men of lesser degree, but He was longsuffering and patient with me. He stayed with me until my freedom came. Even though God was merciful, I suffered significantly for my ignorance, disobedience, and for walking in my flesh and stepping out of the will of God. Even God's people will not escape the sowing and reaping principle.

Regardless of my injuries, how many mistakes I made, or how damaged I was when I came to Christ, I was still my Father's daughter. The King's daughters are unique, and peculiar in character, born of the Spirit, washed in the Blood of the Lamb, and set aside for the Master's use and not for the utilization of the uncircumcised. I am spiritually born of royalty, and God has made me deserving through His Blood of everything of royalty; of the King's best men to the best earthly possessions.

I came to an understanding and realization of God's Word that regardless of what happened to me early on in my life, after I took on the name of Jesus and was filled with His Spirit, my past went down in the grave, and I took on a whole new beginning. My past was washed away as far as God was concerned. I learned some things about the body, soul, and spirit that were paramount to the understanding of some of my past behaviors.

Believers need God's guidance when choosing a spouse because sometimes we are not ready to share our lives with another individual. There are some issues of which God will heal us as we continue in marriage, but some issues need resolving before we get married. God loves His daughters too much to connect them with men who are totally warped and may cause his daughters their demise, and He equally loves his sons too much to connect them with women who are dealing with pre-existing, warped issues that may cause his sons their demise. God knows just when, how, and with whom to bless us. His timing is always perfect, and His choices are always best.

Early on in my life, I was not ready. I thought a companion would be the answer to all of my problems, but it was quite the contrary. I was not prepared to share my life in marriage with a man because my *inner man* was terribly unarranged, confused, and wounded to the extent that I was not psychologically, emotionally, or sexually ready to respond adequately. I needed inner healing. Jesus was the answer to my problems.

SUMMARY

Knowledge of who we are in Christ is critical to our present and future. It is a matter of life and death. Sometimes we become what others say we are because we do not know our identity. Other people will form us if we do not know who we are in Christ. It is just as important to know who we are as well as knowing whose we are. It works like this: If we are aware of who we are, then knowledge to whom we are to listen, trust, follow, and mimic will become apparent. If none of these items are evident, then we will:

- Listen to people who will give us bad advice;
- Trust the people who will use and abuse us because they don't know who we are
- Render our heart and trust to people who have personal agendas for our lives;
- End up in the destiny of someone else because we are going down the wrong path
- And we will mimic the wrong people and end up being someone that God did not design us to be.

Knowing who we are in Christ will help us avoid being manipulated, taken advantage of, abused, misled, or shaped into the image of someone else. Knowing that we are children of the King will keep us focused on how we are to live. Christians have characteristics with which the world is not familiar:

> *But ye are a chosen generation, a royal priesthood, an holy nation, a peculiar people; that ye should shew forth the praises of him who hath called you out of darkness into his marvelous light; (I Peter 2:9)*

Allotted to us are things withheld from the world, and it is because of who we are in Christ.

> *Ye are of God, little children, and have overcome them: because greater is he that is in you, than he that is in the world. (I John 4:4)*

CHAPTER 9

Divine Destiny and Purpose

❦

FROM THE DAY I WAS conceived in my mother's womb, satan had a hit on my life. My mom chose not to abort me, and the war was on:

* nearly died from an unknown sickness at only a few months old
* almost fell into the Mississippi River while riding the ferry from Missouri to Kentucky
* a man who had murdered others in the neighborhood in which we lived broke into our apartment while we were asleep; God let us survive that incident without harm.
* nearly suffered a nervous breakdown in my early twenties
* overdosed on drugs two times during my teenage years
* came very close to death while giving birth to my second daughter; her life was threatened also
* developed high blood pressure and nearly suffered a stroke after giving birth to my last child

One of my most frightening experiences happened in June 1979 while I was living in Chicago, and it was one of the most defining times of when I thought that my life was near over. It happened only a few months before leaving the city life. This is the account as I recall it:

I had been living in Chicago for over a year and a half. Having been raised in a small town, I had not yet become accustomed to the fast pace of city life. My eating habits changed dramatically, I was not getting the proper rest to which I was accustomed, and I was losing weight considerably at one point. I decided to leave the city for a few days and visit my mom. Before leaving Chicago, I began feeling frail in my body and faint in my mind. I arrived at my mom's house on a Friday evening. The following morning, my mom went fishing as she normally did. My mind was becoming more unstable by the hour, and my body grew weaker as the day progressed. Suddenly, something bizarre and horrifying happened. I came to a point where I could feel my mind slip in and out of a place of darkness. I felt as though I was standing on the edge of a mountain, as my body swayed back and forth with the wind. And with every sway of my body, I could feel the closeness of falling off the edge. This drama continued for a few hours. I knew that if God did not help me, I would break.

Realizing that I had not been eating and resting properly, I tried eating, but every time I ingested food, I regurgitated it. I became exhausted, and I thought I might lie down and rest. I went to extreme measures to sleep. Even though I drank a half bottle of Nyquil and took some very powerful sleeping pills, they had no effect on my situation. When I closed my eyes to sleep, I felt as if my eyeballs were rolling over and over in my head. I felt that every nerve in my body was racing—all trying to get out of my body at the same time. I knew at that point that something awful was going to happen to me if I did not get help right away. I went to the ER and explained to the doctor exactly how I was feeling and what had transpired up to that point. I believe the doctor thought that I was on drugs or just plain out of my mind. He did not write out a prescription for me. He did not refer me to another doctor. He did not examine me physically. He did not take my blood pressure or give me a urine test, and he did not give me a diagnosis or prognosis. He only told me to take my daughter to a babysitter and get some rest. Part of my reason for being in the ER was because I could not rest, which is what I relayed to him when I entered his office. I was too weak to argue or contend with him, so I left the hospital and took my daughter to my grandmother's house. I tried once again to sleep, but it became impossible. It was obviously part of God's plan to show me His awesome power, which could not have happened with the doctor's assistance.

My situation grew worse and more intense as the evening progressed. I felt my mind slowly drifting into an area in which I was totally unfamiliar...it was a dark and dismal place. I eventually lost all concept of reasoning and was confused about what was going on around me, and my thinking ability was slowly drifting away. This episode lasted until my mom returned from her fishing trip, which was late in the evening. I was totally unaware when my mother came home that I was wearing only my underwear, and honestly, I was not sane enough to even care.

I tried explaining to my mom what happened during the day. Mentally exhausted, I asked her to take me to the church so that I could pray at the altar and wait to die. I knew that I could not go on in my present condition. I also knew that if I had died, my soul would have been lost. I wanted to get my life right with God before dying. I lost all hope. I thank God, though for a mother who believed in the power of prayer and miracles. The Bible reads:

"The effectual fervent prayer of a righteous man availeth much." (James 5:16)

My mother ministered to my spirit under the power of the Holy Ghost. She told me that I did not have to go to the church and pray because God was there with us. She also encouraged me that I did not have to die in my condition and that God would heal me if I would only have faith. She prayed for me, asking God to have mercy on me. I began praying also. Before very long, I was heavily in prayer. The Holy Spirit took over, and I felt a sensation in my stomach after about twenty minutes of praying to God. I knew then that healing was taking place.

My mom left the room, allowing me to be with God in private. In my prayer to God for healing, I was very honest in expressing to Him that I would not make a promise to give my life to Him after He healed me. I wanted my sanity back at that time, and I knew that no one except God was able to do it. No psychologist or psychiatrist could help me; the doctor had already turned me away. I needed divine intervention. I knew enough about God to know that I could not trick or manipulate Him into healing me, although I was well aware that a person's salvation is God's priority, not just healing. I realize today that I was very bold in telling God what I was not going to do when my very life depended on His mercy. In my heart,

*though, I did want to give my life to Him. I wanted to change, but I didn't
feel that I could because of all of the issues in my life at the time. I was tired
of the life I was living; going from relationship to relationship, and having
abortion after abortion. My very soul was restless and exhausted.*

*I felt the healing power of God move inside of me as I felt strength enter
my body. After a while, my mind slowly returned to normal. I left the bedroom. My mom cooked a nice, healthy meal, and I was able to eat without
regurgitating. As the night progressed, I felt more and more normal. Some
people only talk about God being a mind regulator, but there is nothing
like a personal experience.*

*Later that night, the enemy, my adversary, the devil, tried to steal my
healing, and he would have if allowed to do so. I recall waking up during
the night unable to remember who I was, where I was, or what had transpired during the day. After about one minute or so, I recognized my surroundings. I began rehearsing in my mind the entire day and the events as I
reclaimed my healing and a sound mind, rejecting all thoughts of insanity.
I learned a valuable lesson after that night. I learned that the human spirit
never sleeps. Even in an unconscious state, the spirit is alert and active.
Satan tried to steal my healing victory while I was asleep; however, faith
was locked into my spirit after God healed me, and I went to sleep with
divine assurance and security that God healed me. Satan was unable to
penetrate my faith because faith locked into my spirit.*

Time does not permit me to tell of other attempts satan made on my life,
but God has declared the beginning from the end.

Looking at the way my life began, it appeared as if it would end up
a total disaster. There is a point that my life has already reached in the
mind of God, and the end thereof is already declared. The end was present before the beginning, but before reaching the end, the beginning was
necessary. Events that occurred at the beginning were not the end, and
the beginning could in no way dictate or control what my destiny would
be. The end of what will be is already in motion, and I'm entering it as I
continue moving into my future. Victory and success are guaranteed, and
defeat is not in the script

Despite the evil perpetrated against me during my childhood and young adult years, God was there in every phase and stage. These events (and others that I have not shared) describe my survival of the sexually perverted acts against my body, but it also describes the extraordinary works of God in my soul and spirit. It tells of His love and forgiveness, His mercy and grace, and His everlasting love and commitment to His people.

Summary

On our journey as Christians, we do not know where in this world we will end up. We may eventually end up living our lives in Russia if we were born in Asia. We may very well end up living our last days in China if we were born in America, and so on and so on. However, our destiny is in the hands of God, and we pray that God's will happens in our lives.

The way in which we are born does not dictate the way in which we will die. We are all born sinners, but if we allow God, we will die Christians. Only our Creator determines how or where our destinies rest. He has placed us on the chess board where we need to be, and only He has the authority to move us around. Wherever He places us is where we fit best. We are put in positions to play a part in the kingdom that will benefit the will of God. If we move out of position, not only will we cause ourselves harm, but we cause others harm as well. We are joined fitly as one body, and we all play a part of vital importance.

I will forever be grateful to my mom for having the faith and confidence in God that He answers prayer. It was because of her faith that God healed me when she and I kneeled and prayed to God for the restoration of my mind. And for that, I dedicate this poem to her. I wrote it a few years after that traumatic event.

-When Mama Prayed-

When I was a child, so little indeed-
I remember my mama getting down on her knees;
I did not understand, then, when I'd hear her say,
"Lord, thank you for taking us through one more day;

Always protect us and help us do good-
And love everybody, Lord, just like we should;"
She was so very persistent; she'd pray day and night-
That God would help us and make things all right.

As the years went by, and the months, and the days-
I'd listen for mama to come in and pray;
I'd get so excited when Mama came in,
Because I understood what Mama's prayers meant then.

For I had learned then, that when we were in trouble-
When Mama prayed, God blessed our house double;
When we had no food, and the cupboard was bare,
When Mama prayed, God sent food from somewhere;

When our garments wore out, and our shoes had no soles-
When Mama prayed, God gave us new shoes and clothes;
When we ran out of oil and the coals, they got rare,
After Mama prayed, we had coals and oil to spare;

When the storms came, and the lightning flashed-
When Mama prayed, so quick the storms passed;
When our neighbors and friends treated us wrong-
When Mama prayed, God made us all strong;

When a dear, loved one passed, it caused us much grief,
But when Mama prayed to God, He sent some relief;
It seemed that whenever we encountered great problems-
When Mama prayed, God always solved them.

Growing up at home I'd often hear Mama say,
"Child, whatever you do, always find time to pray;
Cause prayer changes things, and it always will,
God will hear you pray, and your request He will fill.

The memories of Mama's prayers yet linger on-
And some of Mama's prayers I now pray at home;
I've learned the true secret of life's success-
Stay on your knees; God will do the rest.

This poem was written in Chicago in 1979 and revised after I rededicated my life to God.

Divine Destiny and Purpose

In the past, I wondered why I am here-
In this ghastly world of horror and fear;
Never regretting the day I was born-
Cause the reason is thoughtless and so forlorn

I wanted to know why life exists-
On a planet so filled with a dusty mist;
I related my dream to a place so divine-
Where people were genuine, honest, and kind

As I lived throughout each troublesome day-
Worries and wishes led the way;
I tried to find some peace of mind,
I fought vigorously to leave my past behind;

I hoped someday to understand-
Why God created mortal man;
I tried to convey the reason why-
All who sin will surely die;

But now that I know my true destiny,
And since the day Christ set me free-
I no longer wonder why I am here-
Cause my purpose in life God has made very clear.

Who hath saved us, and called us with an holy calling, not according to our works, but according to his own purpose and grace, which was given us in Christ Jesus before the world began. (II Timothy 1:9)

CHAPTER 10

The Transformation Begins

⋘⧉⋙

I MOVED FROM ILLINOIS TO Ohio in 1999. In January 2000, God strategically placed me in the ministry of one of the greatest apostles of our time. I have no doubt that God graced me when He directed me to such a leader. It was another one of His ways of showing me that He is truly in control, knows just what I need, and gives me only His very best.

My spiritual life flourished in such a phenomenal and indescribable way. The Word of God was copiously rich and ministered with such power and illumination that it transformed and revolutionized my life. I cannot pinpoint the exact minute or hour that I was healed and set free, but over the course and process of time, and as the Word of God touched and penetrated those sensitive areas, deliverance became inevitable. Illumination of God's Word caused me to stand erect and speak those things that are not as though they were.

God unfolded mysteries to me concerning my issues as my pastor taught, preached, ministered, prophesied, and prayed. God instructed me on what to do and how to do it. I felt many times as if I was sitting at the feet of Jesus and getting instructions on how to overcome, gain a positive self- perception, and walk in victory. God did send other powerful, anointed and experienced prophets to speak into my life and confirm the things He was ministering to me and had shown me through dreams and visions.

I researched the effects that sexual abuse, rape, and incest have on children. I have read many articles, books, and journals. I've searched the internet and talked to many men and women of which we have had the same experiences. In all of my research, reading, and conversations with other victors, I had my experience to confirm what I have read, studied, and heard. I must admit that I did fit the description of much of what clinicians have described and reported about the effects that sexual abuse has on children. I have concluded that transformation and healing are possible when one has been traumatized.

Some clinicians lack the faith that God heals traumatized and sexually abused victims. From some of the documentaries, journals, and books that I have read, this appears especially true in the area of psychiatry and psychology. There were times during my studies that I struggled to maintain my faith in the power of God to heal sick minds; but I concluded in all of my research and studies that no matter what we encounter in life, God is still God. No illness, dysfunction or mental instability is too hard for Him to heal. I came to this conclusion because I experienced it for myself. With or without medication, psychiatrists, and psychologists, God **can** and **does** heal, and He doesn't need to counsel with doctors or anyone in the medical field to perform the miraculous. He has never needed medication to get the job done, and He never will. I acknowledge and appreciate the many breakthroughs in the field of medicine and psychology, but I will never cease to acknowledge the power of God that can change the lives of people with the mention of His name and the power of His Blood.

Since my transformation, I do not need acclamation from a man to make me feel whole. My focus is not on finding a husband, but it is in my relationship with Jesus Christ and Him fulfilling His purpose for my life. If God chooses to grace me with one of His humble male servants, then I shall be quite grateful to Him; however, if He chooses to have me remain as one of His faithful unmarried daughters, then I shall rejoice, nevertheless because I know that Father knows best.

SUMMARY
The Word of God tells us in Romans 12:2

> *And be not conformed to this world: but be ye transformed by the renewing of your mind, that ye may prove what is that good, and acceptable, and perfect, will of God.*

Transformation is an on-going process. Being transformed is what causes Christians to become what God has designed.

Some of my childhood experiences formed the way in which I perceived men, sex, relationships, marriage, and who I was. My mind was molded to believe that I was not worthy of a man of God as a husband; that I was not good enough for anything positive to happen in my life, and that I had done too much wrong for forgiveness. I needed a complete overhaul of my way of thinking after I became a Christian. I am being renewed in my mind, and I am becoming perfected as I walk with God.

CHAPTER 11

Understanding Child Sexual Abuse

HIDDEN INSIDE THE WALLS OF our country is a menacing evil that seems to prevail despite efforts put forth by agencies, reports, and research. That menacing evil is called *childhood sexual abuse*. Many individuals suffer ineffable trauma due to the lack of attention given to the issue

I feel compelled to provide some vital information about child sexual abuse (CSA), rape, and molestation for those who are unaware of the effects. [1]According to one study, CSA "includes unwanted and inappropriate sexual solicitation of, or exposure to, a child by an older person; genital touching or fondling; or penetration regarding oral, anal or vaginal intercourse or attempted intercourse."

When these definitions are combined and broken down, CSA falls under one of three areas:

1) Molestation: the touching or fondling of the genitals of a child; asking/forcing a child to touch or fondle an adult's genitals; using a child to enhance one's sick pleasure from sexual acts, or pornography
2) Sexual intercourse: which includes vaginal, oral, or rectal penetration of a child
3) Rape: forceful sex with a child

According to the [2]APA, approximately 1 in 6 boys and 1 in four girls experience sexual abuse before they reach age 18. In one [3]Clinical Psychology article, "women who experienced sexual abuse as a child are 2 to 3 times more likely to be sexually assaulted later in life. [4]One in seven youth Internet users received an unwanted sexual solicitation in 2006. [5]According to the U.S. Department of Health and Human Services, in 2012, 62,939 cases of CSA were reported. [6]About 2.78 million men in the United States have been victims of sexual assault or rape. [7]And finally, it is estimated that there are 60 million survivors of CSA living in America.

Some issues and disturbances of CSA that I have personally experienced and have been documented by Clinicians include:

1. A broken body
2. A broken will
3. A broken spirit (mental disorders)
4. Other issues such as:
   a. Alcohol and drug abuse
   b. Running away from home
   c. Prostitution
   d. Promiscuity at an early age
   e. Low self-perception

An examination of each of these matters concludes that CSA is a severe epidemic. CSA brings about enormous devastation in epic proportions.

1. **When a female is abused sexually, her body becomes broken.**
Every female is born with a hymen. [8]The hymen is a thin piece of mucosal tissue surrounding and partially covering the vaginal opening and [9]may become ruptured by sexual intercourse and several other means. When the hymen breaks during sexual intercourse, it causes the expulsion of blood and a watery substance to flow from the vagina. This substance is "the token" of her virginity as described in the Bible in Deuteronomy 22:15-17.

Then shall the father of the damsel, and her mother, take and bring forth the tokens of the damsel's virginity unto the elders of the city in the gate: And the damsel's father shall say unto the elders, I gave my daughter unto this man to wife, and he hateth her; And, lo, he hath given occasions of speech against her saying, I found not thy daughter a maid; and yet, these are the tokens of my daughter's virginity. And they shall spread the cloth before the elders of the city.

People in the Old Testament of the Bible took precautionary measures which gave assurance that women were not put away by false accusations that she was not a virgin at marriage. The parents could take the bed cloth of their wedding night and spread it before the elders of the city as proof that their daughter was pure before marriage.

The breaking of the hymen establishes a blood covenant between the male and the female which states in essence that they are only to engage in sexual intercourse with each other the remaining days of their lives and that a third party never has and will never come between them and their blood covenant. When a female child suffers sexual abuse, her hymen becomes obstructed, her body violated, and her virginity destroyed. She has been physically forced to enter into a blood covenant that she had no power in choosing to or not to enter. She is physically and forcefully stripped of her chastity. Destruction of her virginity can never be retrieved. Her body is violated in the worse way possible.

There are other ways in which the hymen breaks other than by intercourse, but in the context to which I am referring, when a female is raped or sexually assaulted, the hymen becomes disrupted in an illegal, demeaning, and demonic fashion. It causes a broken body.

2. When children are sexually abused, their will becomes violated.

Forcing someone to perform any act against their will is in operation with the spirit of witchcraft. The spirit of witchcraft involves force; coercion; the exercise of power and control over another person's mind and will; it is the use of manipulation, deception, intimidation, lying, and the person's physical, emotional, mental, and intellectual vulnerabilities. It also includes taking advantage of a person's ignorance. [10]It was pointed out by one clinician that "a primary motivation for sexual abusers is power and that sexual gratification is the secondary gain that reinforces the primary behavior."

3. <u>When children are sexually abused, their spirits become broken</u>

[11]In one survey, it was reported that sexually abused females were three times more likely to develop psychiatric disorders than females who were not.

One coping mechanism used by victims of sexual abuse is dissociation. Dissociation is a disorder that is associated with the spirit of man and develops during a time of extreme trauma. It happens when the injury becomes overwhelmingly unbearable for the inner man. It becomes a breaking point and causes the person to transfer the pain to another individual, place, or thing.

In the clinical arena, according to the [12]Canadian Mental Health Association, 97% of dissociative identity disorder (DID) is formed through dissociation. It can exist in sexually abused victims, and it develops when the child splits into two or more personalities as a way to cope with extreme physical, sexual, or psychological abuse. [13]Ross describes dissociation as "a little girl imagining that the abuse is happening to someone else." In his description, the damage is so intense, overbearing, and overwhelming that the little girl dissociates herself and projects the pain onto another imaginary individual. In my situation, I dismissed my body parts into the tunnel to escape the pain and to protect my spirit. It is the mercy and power of God that I did not remain inside the tunnel and another identity formed. For this, I am truly and forever grateful.

In the religious arena, disorders such as DID and Post Traumatic Stress Disorder (PTSD) are sometimes considered demonic in nature. Some theologians, such as conservative Protestants believe that DID and other disorders do not stem from sexual abuse or any other trauma, but that it is a demonic spirit that needs casting out as demonstrated by Jesus during His earthly ministry (Mark 1:34). However, other Christian counselors and theologians have concluded that all personality disorders are not demonic in nature, but some of the activities associated with the disorder may be demonic.

[14]In a published research on the effects of CSA, a meta-analysis revealed that PTSD was listed as one of the outcomes of CSA. [15]There is

evidence that CSA survivors are at risk of psychological, behavioral, and sexual disorders. [16]According to Maltz, CSA can hinder healthy social growth and cause many other psychosocial problems.

I must point out that every abused person may not develop every psychological disorder. I must also say that sexual assault is not the only trauma from which DID or dissociation produces.

4. <u>Other Issues:</u>
A. Alcohol and Drug Abuse
Some sexually abused victims abuse alcohol and drugs as painkillers to help them cope with the trauma. When effects of sexual assault go unresolved, it can very easily result in relapse for those who are recovering from alcohol and drug dependency. Every issue has an origin. Destroying the origin is the beginning of the end of the addiction. [17]Putnam claims that CSA is a significant risk factor for depression and substance abuse. [18]Kenneth Kendler indicates that "…overall, childhood sexual abuse was more strongly associated with drugs or alcohol dependence than any of the psychiatric disorders." The mental disorders described by Kindler included major depression, generalized anxiety disorder, panic disorder, bulimia nervosa, and alcohol and drug dependency. Another report by [19]Simpson states that sexually abused females are three times more likely to report substance abuse than those who have not been sexually abused (40.5% versus 14%).

B. Running Away
When a child runs away from home, individual indicators should be examined. One of those indicators is sexual abuse. Some teenagers experience rebellion and a host of other issues when they are transitioning from child to teen; however, some teens run away from home because of physical, emotional, or sexual abuse. Some run away from home because they have been misused in the past and are imbalanced in their emotions. [20]The NCSL indicates that 17% of run-away youth reported being "forced into unwanted sexual activity by a family or household member." [21]A statistic by the Department of Justice estimated that nearly 450,000 children run away from home every year.

The [22]American Journal of Family Therapy reports that inappropriate family boundaries, along with school performance, relationships with parents, and divorce are themes to discuss with runaway adolescents. Inappropriate family boundaries include sexual abuse and sexual molestation. Moreover, it was asserted that [23]"youth who have been sexually abused often report running away at earlier ages than runaway and homeless youth who report never having been sexually abused."

C. Promiscuity

Victims of CSA have a much higher tendency to become promiscuous at an earlier age than those who are not victims. [24]One mental health study revealed that young females who are forced to have sex are three times more likely to develop psychological disorders than those who are not forced to have sex. Promiscuity is not an unusual behavior of sexually abused children because of their introduction to sex at an early age (some sooner than others). [25]According to Noll, female adult sexually abused survivors are more likely to be sexually promiscuous. [26]The U.S. Census Bureau indicated that in 2008, 41% of all births were to unwed mothers.

D. Low Self-Perception

[27]Victims of CSA often harbor a sense of low self-perception. Many feel defective, unfit, worthless, and useless as indicated by Long. [28]Ratican suggests that some survivors of CSA exhibit dirty or ugly body images and dissatisfaction with their body or appearance, eating disorders and obesity. [29]One study indicated that "usually a child who is the victim of prolonged sexual abuse develops low self-esteem, a feeling of self-worthlessness and an abnormal perspective on sexuality."

It is imaginative that females who are dealing with feelings of rejection, self-worthlessness, and low self-perception would feel useless in the upkeep of their bodies. [30]A journal of Child Abuse and Neglect indicates that "middle aged women who were sexually abused as children were twice as likely to be diagnosed with an eating disorder compared to women who were not sexually abused as children."

Summary

The emotional pain, suffering, trauma, torment, and terror that victims of CSA endure are devastating to the human soul and can be just as destructive to the human body and spirit. The evil that is perpetrated by sexual deviance has turned many little girls and boys into runaways, alcohol and drug abusers, prostitutes, multiples and promiscuous individuals. The emotional trauma developed can and often follow them throughout their adolescence and adulthood, and even sometimes to their graves. For an experience to inhabit an individual's soul over so long a period and cause such irreversible damage and devastation, it has to have a powerful and controlling impact.

I am in no way implying that CSA is the only pretext for the behaviors listed, however, being a survivor of such trauma, I understand how these actions are triggered. The pain and suffering of the abuse can be so intense that its effects can last for years after the abuse has desisted.

Please note that the disorders described do not necessarily suggest that every child that experience them are sexual abuse victims, although some are strong indicators that abuse is present or has happened. Also, some disorders that survivors of CSA experience are not mentioned in this chapter. The disorders in this section are a basis for those who are not aware of the effects of CSA. It is not meant to make anyone panic or become overly suspicious of neighbors, family, friends, or relatives.

The problem of CSA is that although it is an old issue, it is also a growing concern for researchers, clinicians, clergy, and other professionals who continue to study and unveil its causes and effects.

Victims of CSA can also become victors. As serious as the problem is in this country, it is not given as much attention as it should, in my opinion. Some entities and policymakers are not interested or compassionate enough to take on the challenge. The Church community needs to get more involved in the issue of CSA. However, many groups and organizations are struggling to find more ways to get the issue into the public and to those who can make a more powerful impact and contribute more to solving the problem. For instance, in June 2011, President Obama announced a new [31]<u>Father and Mentoring Initiative</u> "to engage individuals and organizations in responsible parenting and improve city and state community programs that offer services such as parenting classes."

The court system has much to bear in the area of punishment and helping to keep the perpetrators off the streets and in counseling, instead of giving lenient sentences to the perpetrators. A lack of strong convictions from the courts sends a message to perpetrators that they can commit the crime and do little or no time. It is my assumption that because the male gender dominates the tribunal, there are less and shorter sentences to the perpetrators and there is less sensitivity to the issue.

The Male Gender and Child Sexual Abuse

✦

THERE IS A STRONG POSSIBILITY that at least four of the men with whom I was involved were victims of CSA. I am sure that one of them was a victim. Church, community, friends, family and other entities are sometimes reluctant to initiate the conversation about sexual abuse. When sexual assault happens to a male, at times communication and report of the incident may surface, but in most situations, very quickly, it vanishes.

The relationships between sexual assault and sexual risk, substance use, emotional stress, and conduct problems were examined among 190 runaways in a study. [1]The study indicated that "males abused before age 13 had more sexual partners than those not abused and runaways were significantly more likely to have been sexually abused than has been reported in prior research." [2]Research has shown that the sexual abuse of boys is more prevalent than believed. [3]Research also indicates that men are less likely to disclose the abuse during childhood than women and that [4]64% of women compared to 26% of men exposed the abuse when they were children.

Infestation of sexual perversion is tearing our country down. [5]McBride reported that one in every six males are victims of CSA. The same article describes many of these men as living with the problem of debilitating and shattered trust. A report by [6]Central Minnesota Sexual Assault Center indicated that 2.78 million men in the United States are victims of sexual assault or rape.

There is much research on effects that CSA has on men. [7]One research carried out on male sexual abuse concludes that hospitalization of boys for psychiatric treatment is at a higher rate than girls. [8]Another research found that sexually abused boys experienced more emotional and behavioral problems than females; suicide is one of the behavioral problems. [9]As described by the Public Health Agency of Canada, it is common for men who have experienced CSA to experience difficulty with reaching an orgasm or to have an erection. [10]Evidence suggests that more male victims have experienced "same-sex molestation than female victims, greater violence, and physical harm during the abuse, and are more likely to have been victimized by multiple perpetrators. [11]Another article reveals that "there is evidence of inter-generational effects from abused parents, mediated through anxiety and mental health problems and parenting stresses."

SUMMARY

CSA, as we can see, has no particular face, race, gender, financial, or social status. [12]As documented by one study, children who live in rural areas are twice as likely to be identified as victims of sexual abuse than those living in urban areas. Boys are victims as well as girls and suffer just as much trauma as their female counterparts. Churches and other institutions owe it to children to do an adequate job of protecting them from the rash of sexual abuse. Every entity possible needs to come together and assist in meeting the needs of sexually abused children.

If you are a male and reading this book, please be assured that you are not alone if you have been sexually assaulted or sexually abused as a child. Finding a support group, seeking counsel, or telling someone will possibly release some of the pressure; however, bringing the problem to the light is the initial step that you must take. There is hope for your situation!

CHAPTER 13

Child Sexual Abuse from a Spiritual Perspective

WHILE WORKING THROUGH MY ISSUES of trauma, I always knew that there was something strange going on in my life that was far beyond my imagination, my comprehension, this physical world, or my ability to deal with the issue alone. I knew that I loved God, wanted to be a true Christian, to be holy, clean, pure, and righteous. In spite of all that I desired to be, I had this "thing" hanging over my head and operating in my life. I had a feeling of something being very "wrong."

When an individual becomes born again, their spirit quickens (comes alive). The spirit of God enters their spirit, and they come alive. When the Bible says that we are born again, we are born again of water and spirit.

Jesus answered, Verily, verily, I say unto thee, Except a man be born of water and of the Spirit, he cannot enter into the kingdom of God. (John 3:5)

The law of the LORD is perfect (flawless), restoring and refreshing the soul; The statutes of the LORD are reliable and trustworthy, making wise the simple. (Psalms 19:7, Amplified)

The soulish arena consists of the mind, the will, the emotions, and the intellect. In respect to this description of the tripartite, I knew that I was born again, and God's Spirit resided in me. I was still in my human body, and my soul was the entity of the three parts that was in distress. My body was healthy, but my soul was in a state of being saved. My soul needed converting and my mind needed a transformation. Memories of my past haunted and tormented my mind. I did not know how to rid myself of these thoughts, feelings, emotions, and the trauma that was attached. So, what do we do when we do not know what to do? We go to our Father. I went to my Father and asked Him what I should do about the memories, the trauma, the hurt, the pain, and of course, the dreams.

The very first thing that the Spirit of God had me do was to forgive all those who had harmed me. I forgave all the guys that cheated on me, raped me, molested me and took advantage of me. That action freed me of some space. It was like having an overload on the computer and getting rid of some of the unwanted programs to make room for other programs. Forgiveness replaced un-forgiveness. What I did not understand at the time was that the enemy used the men in my life to try to destroy me and to stop me from reaching my destiny. He uses us all in one form or another if we are willing vessels.

God says that He knew us before we were formed in the womb. An example is John the Baptist. The angel told Zacharias that his wife would give birth to a son, and he shall be filled with the Holy Ghost in his mother's womb, and so it was *(Luke 1:15)*. Just as a child can be filled with the Holy Ghost in the womb, a child can also be filled with other spirits in the womb.

The enemy sets us up at birth and childhood with traumas and issues, thinking that we will not be able to make it through them, thus stopping our destinies or crippling our abilities to be fruitful and victorious. Most of the things that shape our futures happen to us in our childhood.

As suggested by [1]Frank and Ida Mae Hammond, "when a child does not have satisfactory love relationships in life he grows up being unable to feel and share in love relationships." They also claim that withdrawn type of personality exists with rejection in which lies a starvation of love, insecurity, inferiority, fantasy, and unreality. In essence, childhood is when it all begins.

The enemy can enter into our lives when there is an open door. The weakest time of a human's life is childhood. Children cannot protect themselves and are at the mercy of their parents. Molestation, rape, and incest are doors that the enemy uses to come in and take up habitation in a child's life. When these spirits come in, they do not come alone. They bring others with them. Physical abuse, emotional abuse, neglect, rejection, and abandonment are major doors in a child's life through which demonic spirits enter.

Principles that we learn in life help to shape our decisions, and the things we do. Even though the Holy Spirit lived inside of me, some things had shaped my thinking (mind) before I was born again. Those things had to change so that I could fully commit to God and even to obey Him. They ranged anywhere from feeling unwanted and unloved, to emotionally deprived and useless.

"And do not be conformed to this world [any longer with its superficial values and customs], but be transformed and progressively changed [as you mature spiritually] by the renewing of your mind [focusing on godly values and ethical attitudes], so that you may prove [for yourselves] what the will of God is, that which is good and acceptable and perfect [in His plan and purpose for you]. (Romans 12:2 Amplified)

[2]The Greek word in this context for the word "transformed" means "Metamorphosis" which refers to the process that leads to an outward, permanent change.

Even though I felt that God loved me, it was imperative that I trusted Him enough to allow Him to enter into those deep, dark places in my soul. When we give our lives to God, we must give him everything. Everything means everything! We must be willing to share even the darkest, most hurtful and disturbing things. And we must be prepared to leave those places when the spirit is trying to pull us away. My transformation did not happen overnight. I had made more mistakes before I was free of the pain and all of the other emotions.

There are many hurting females (and males) in church ministries and professional positions that are still living in a state of need. Many of them are in need of deliverance. One reason there is so much contention, strife, confusion, and other elements of a fleshly nature operating inside of ministries, sometimes, is because people are dealing with anger, hurt, and pain, and are trying to prove themselves. They are exercising power and control over other people (which are elements of the power of witch-craft), insecurities (which can be signs of rejection), and ego problems (which deals with pride).

As Christians, we need to step back and ask God if we have honestly considered, or allowed Him to deal with our issues. Sometimes problems of having been abused sexually, physically, or emotionally cause grown-ups to act out just as it does children. If a female is a sexually abused vic-tim, she needs to be set free before trying to lead another group of women (or men). If she has not faced the issue and is not free of it, it is imperative that she does so that she can have a successful life and ministry.

I believe that most women are honestly in their positions because God has placed them there, and their intentions and motives are pure. The reality is that these things do exist in the body of Christ and they need addressing. Many Christian people are suffering at the hands of leaders and think that it is God's will that they remain in an individual congrega-tion. They do not realize that sometimes they are dealing with leaders who have unresolved childhood issues that are causing the problem. They may have demons that need casting out because their issue may be of a demonic nature, but Demons cannot be counseled, and they do not come out through therapy.

It is not to say that ALL women who have experienced sexual abuse as children are dealing with the same problems. But it is beyond a reasonable doubt that they are dealing with a psychological problem or behavior that is demon-orchestrated if they are exercising what I have described above, and those problems have triggers. For example, if a female is leading a ministry and she has not dealt with the rape or incest that happened in her childhood, she may have a problem with rejection or low self-perception. If low self-perception is her issue, she may be intimidated by men and may try to block them from exercising their gifts or from operating fully in ministry. If the issue is rejection, she may try very hard to prove herself even to the point of overexertion. Many problems can result after being molested, and being a leader in the church in any capacity is a very dangerous thing if the problem remains unresolved.

SUMMARY

When Christians do not deal with their issues, it becomes a severe and long-standing problem in the body of Christ. Many need to search their hearts, come clean, get rid of their pride and ego, and go before God for healing.

Just as females have problems, Christian men who were sexually abused as children also need to come clean. How many times have we read about or seen men of God who have molested boys and girls or slept with multiple women in the church? How many times have we heard of, read about, or known pastors or ministers who have children out of wedlock with other women in the church? These are sexually perverted problems that could have stemmed from the men having been molested or raped when they were children. But it is hard to know because the church isn't talking about it on the level that it should. Not once in my Christian life have I experienced a ministry in a church that deals with sexually abused children. If they are out there, then, that is a beautiful thing.

The secular world has many programs, hotlines, and organizations that deal with issues of CSA. We don't have to follow the world, but there needs to be a place where men, women, and children can receive help for their problems. Demons may not have inhabited all sexually abused children and adults, but it is certain that some have. There needs to be a place in the ministry that can assist the men, women, and children who are victims of CSA.

Child Sexual Abuse from a Clinical/Psychological Perspective

THE TOUCH FACTOR

IN RESEARCHING EFFECTS OF CSA, I stumbled upon an article written by Dr. Ben Benjamin. [1] The article expressed that in hospitals across America, premature infants and infants isolated in sterile environments are given the touch therapy of massage for fifteen minutes, three times a day. The article further stipulated that "touch is vital for survival in the very young." It is of great importance that parents give their children emotional support by embracing, kissing, rubbing, smiling, and exercising other loving gestures that give children a sense of acceptance, acclamation, and affirmation. When omitted, children will automatically seek them out in other places because humans need these elements to survive.

THE POWER

Women who thirst to gain positions that place them in authority over men could be operating in the spirit of sublimation. [2] Sublimation is "a mature type of defense mechanism where socially unacceptable impulses or idealizations are unconsciously transformed into socially acceptable actions or behavior, possibly resulting in a long-**term** conversion of the initial impulse." In other words, sublimation is expressing unacceptable social drives in ways that are acceptable. A good example of this is if a woman wants to get back at a man for hurting her, she may climb the social ladder in a corporation with the full intent of managing men to destroy them. She may work her way into a position of power, and there she has the authority to fire them for the smallest thing. Her position of power and authority in the corporation is socially acceptable. Firing someone is socially acceptable behavior. Getting a gun, entering a mall, and killing a mass number of men is not socially acceptable behavior. The most socially acceptable approach is to reach a plateau where she has authority over men and then hurt them by not promoting them; communicating with them with disrespect and contempt and making them feel that they are beneath her. These actions make her feel a sense of empowerment. As far as the Body of Christ goes, every woman in the church may not fall into this category, but women who are dealing with unresolved issues need to give attention to the issue and somehow get it resolved.

PSYCHE ISSUES

Effects of sexual abuse on children are phenomenal. Many victims grow up spending much of their lives trying to overcome the pain and memories. [3]Some professionals and some public figures believe that sexual abuse of children can result in multiple personality disorders, problems within relationships, PTSD, depression, eating disorders, and anxiety. Other professionals and clinicians have diagnosed many disorders and dysfunctions and linked them to CSA. [4]One researcher indicated that PTSD is now associated with not only war victims, but any person who has experienced extreme trauma, including CSA. Any trauma that is so unbearable to the human psyche that it causes a change in one's course of life or causes an inability to function in society can be identified and labeled as PTSD.

Sexual violence against children cost America millions of dollars. Their physical bodies and their psychological health are on the line and demand attention. [5]According to one report, sexually violent crimes against children ages 0-14 cost $71 billion a year; sexually violent crimes against children 15-24 cost $45 billion a year, and the average cost of mental health care for each sexual abuse victim is $5,800. It is apparent from this report that there is a significant problem with CSA in America.

Summary

Whether sexual abuse has a clinical or psychological attachment, it doesn't lessen the pain, hurt, guilt, shame, or embarrassment that goes along with it. Clinicians have their ideologies and theologians also have their perspectives; however, when summarized, CSA causes many issues from struggling to overcome the effects to living a life of sexual confusion and dysfunction. America's apathy to challenge itself to come to the aid of sexually abused children is what perpetuates the crime.

Soul Murder

SOUL MURDER HAPPENS WHEN A child is abused sexually, mentally, physically or emotionally. It is when a child is neglected or deprived of the joys of life so much so that it destroys the child's soul. It is deprivation in raw form. The soul becomes limp and unresponsive to individual elements of life. It is a sad and gloomy cave-like existence that only comes to the surface to experience torment, pain, and suffering.

Although it seems that sexual and physical abuse is reported in greater numbers, emotional abuse has just as much a devastating effect on a child as the other types of ill-treatments. Emotional abuse has a different element than other childhood injuries. Unlike physical violence, emotional abuse is not confirmed with the naked eye. However, emotional and mental damages are ill-treatments that live in the mind and soul. [1]In an article by [1]Vachss, it is demonstrated that emotional abuse is like cancer which can be seen only on the inside but manifested by physical signs.

[2]According to Hutchison and Mueller, emotional abuse results in future victimization, low self-esteem, passivity, and a sad feeling of self-esteem. They also stipulate that emotional abuse includes rejection by parents, condemnation, voice elevation, slapping, nagging, and threats. The level of low self-esteem, according to the study, can result in an inability to become successful. Many of these actions by parents are belittling to a child and cause feelings of withdrawal and other emotions that isolate them from other peers, people, social activities, and friends.

It is imperative that parents bond with their children. Bonding is demonstrated by parents taking the time to hug their children, kiss them on their forehead, and stroke them physically. Bonding can also be expressed by parents telling their kids that they love them, smiling at them, saying things that are encouraging, listening to them, and showing affection. Without these elements in a child's life, unless God comes along through some other means and rescues them, doom and failure are inevitable.

SUMMARY

Sometimes it is very hard to accept issues that underline our lives. Honesty is the most effective characteristic to exercise when trying to overcome any problem. Lies, deceit, denial, and ignoring the issue prolong the healing process.

CHAPTER 16

Disconnecting Music from the Soul

⬥⬥⬥

LOADED IN THE LIBRARY OF our conscious and subconscious is an entourage of songs and music that are attached to an event, era, moment, time, place, or person. We can associate some songs with an entire season in our lives. When we hear certain songs, memories are displayed in movie form, and the events, places, people, or things, are activated in our souls. The way in which they affect us depends on whether the situation was pleasant, traumatic, sad, happy, or other. The entities of our being that were active— such as the color or type of clothes worn, the time of day— all provoke the key to the memory.

Love, hate, happiness, fear, pain, desire and other emotions can connect with a song. If a certain song were playing during a certain time or event in which one of these emotions were happening, that song would forever be associated and connected with that particular emotion. The mind subconsciously and consciously remembers the feeling. [1]Dr. Jäncke suggests that "emotional music we have heard at specific periods of our life is strongly linked to our *autobiographical memory* and thus is intimately involved in forming our view of our self."

[2]Autobiographical memory is "a memory system consisting of episodes recollected from an individual's life, based on a combination of episodic (personal experiences and specific objects, people, and events experienced at particular times and places) and semantic (general knowledge and facts about the world) **memory**."

Putting this knowledge together, I understood why some songs made me think about J. I also knew how important it was for me to stop listening to certain songs altogether. But it was tough to do so because some of the songs made me feel warm and loved, the way that J made me feel. During my relationship with J, several songs became my favorites. I played them repeatedly. They became part of my soul experience with him. The music was my connection to him. And this is how it worked. Listening to music is a gratifying experience and causes a neurotransmitter in the brain called dopamine to be released. [3]Dopamine is associated with the pleasure system of the brain that provides feelings of enjoyment and reinforcement to motivate us to continue a particular activity; it is released by rewarding experiences such as eating food, having sex, and even taking certain nonprescription drugs. Playing certain songs over and over kept me connected with J because of the reward of the good feeling I received.

My relationship with J was very pleasant, and listening to the songs that made me think of him released high doses of dopamine because the feelings were great. The songs connected to my soul, and every time I heard them or listened to them, my mind traveled back to the place with J where I felt secure and loved. *Make Me Yours* by Betty Swann was the leading song that kept me connected with J. The song engraved the good feeling I got the day he stood for me at school; that was a defining moment in my life and one that I remembered for many years. Hearing and singing *Make Me Yours* at any given time released large doses of dopamine, which kept me desiring, not J, but the type of relationship we shared. Memories from the past flooded my mind and continually drew me back to some of the scenes, actions, and activities that we shared. Even now, I must be very careful that I do not allow doors to open that will take me back, and listening to that song may trigger a door.

There was a song that I loved to hear my mother sing when I was younger. It always made me think of Dad, and from what I remember, that particular song was one of Dad's favorites. When I grew older, I sang the song myself because it made me think of him. But that was before he passed away. After he passed away and I sang the song, it made me feel sorrowful because he was no longer here. One day, while singing the song and thinking about Dad, the Lord ministered to me to stop singing the song. It was not easy for me to let go because I had sung the song for many years. I recovered from the grief and was able to move on with my life. But it only happened after I stopped singing the song; continuing to sing the song prolonged my recovery.

Music and memory are a very powerful duo. They assist us in maintaining a connection with the past. The past is not always a good thing of which to hold on, especially when the memories keep us locked into a place, time, or era, stifle our growth, trigger bad memories, or disable us from moving forward.

CHAPTER 17

The Healing Process

〰️

MANY PEOPLE OVERCOME TRAUMA BY different means. My victory came through dreams and visions, praying, listening to the Word of God through various ministers, being watchful and discerning, and being alert of things that were happening in my life. The victory came to me through these steps:

* Step one was to **acknowledge** that an issue existed.

I found out that it was perfectly okay to verbally acknowledge that there was something wrong, even though it didn't feel pleasant. It took humility to admit it. To know that there is a problem and to allow the words to come forth out of the mouth are two different things with two different results. To be honest and transparent is to acknowledge that a problem exists. Verbally admitting that there is a problem breaks pride down.

"Pride goeth before destruction, and a haughty spirit before a fall." (Proverbs 16:18)

* Step two was to **identify** the issue.

God clearly revealed to me what was going on in my life. He revealed to me that I needed to know and believe that He loved me. Even though I was a Christian when my healing began, and I had the Holy Spirit living inside of me, I needed freedom from all the things that made me feel unloved.

The list was very long. I was worshiping and praising God, telling Him how much I loved Him and even believing most of the time that I was loved, but other times, I felt unloved deep down in my soul. Memories of the past rape, the molestation, the abandonment, and rejection that I felt as a child all were nesting in my soul. I had no friends that I could talk to because I disassociated myself from them when I became a Christian.

The church never addressed issues of CSA on any level; although some of the women attending had been raped and molested. Many had rejection and abandonment issues and were operating out of pain and hurt, and most of the time it was apparent. It was my responsibility to get healed and delivered. The journey was long and painful, but victorious.

* Step three was to **forgive** everyone who had ever hurt or harmed me.

I forgave the people who hurt me, rejected me, abandoned me, molested and raped me. I recall praying many times and calling out the names of those involved. It brought cleansing to my soul. It was like cleaning house and getting rid of all the spider webs, dust balls, dirt, and grime.

* Step four was to stop looking for someone to love me and **focus** on getting healed and raising my children.

I moved from Ohio to Illinois in 1999 where the healing process went full force. My focus shifted from the hurt and pain to searching for God's will, plan, and purpose for my life. During that time is when the Holy Spirit showed me many dreams and visions, through which came part of my healing, knowledge, revelation, and freedom. One vision vividly stands out in my mind. In the vision, I got out of my bed, pulled back the cover, and there I saw the head of a woman. Wrapped around her head was a bandana. The woman looked up at me with a grin on her face. I immediately started speaking to the head and ran it out of the apartment. But I noticed that the door was cracked, and it was easy for the head to leave. That was the end of the dream. I had a conversation with one of the ministers of the church, and we agreed that the head symbolized generations. I believe that God was showing me that I was dealing with a generational issue. The things that I experienced as a child did not begin with me. Four generations of my family had dealt with molestation, rape, and incest, and included males and females.

There were other times when I was asleep during the night and felt things moving under the covers in my bed. I would always rebuke the spirit of perversion and call on the Blood of Jesus and the name of Jesus. Before moving to Ohio, I had a recurring dream of dogs and foxes chasing me, but before they could get inside the house, I would somehow get the door closed. This recurring dream persisted for many years. Dreams about the dogs and foxes dissipated after I was healed and set free. I had been celibate for many years and was focusing on my life with Christ before I knew it. After going through the troubled times of my life, I discerned that I had developed patterns of getting married every six years.

Sometimes, God has to take us to a different physical location for healing. I did not question God as to why He wanted me to relocate before my deliverance came. Years later I understood. I needed a change in atmospheres. It was relevant to my healing that I surrounded myself with apostles, prophets, and men and women of God with power and authority. I needed to sit under the teaching and preaching that could help my state of mind and keep me focused and busy with the things of God.

CHAPTER 18

The Scar is Proof that the Wound has Healed

EMOTIONAL AND PHYSICAL PAINS SHARE some of the same elements. One of the differences is the means by which the pain is perpetrated. Only the scar remains when both physical and emotional healing has taken place. A scar and a wound cannot exist at the same time.

A physical injury hurts when it is touched because it still has soreness. It still has feelings as long as it is a wound. It is still a wound even when it is not agitated by touch. The wound has healed when there is no pain. Just as a physical wound has healed when there is no pain or soreness, an emotional wound has healed when the tears cease to flow from the memory, forgiveness has taken place, and fear has subsided.

After God healed me, I no longer cried when I spoke or thought about the past. Although I am healed, and I no longer cry from the pain, I will always remember what happened. It is a chapter that is part of my life's journey. But it was not meant to consume my life or determine what would be my final destiny.

CHAPTER 19

The Survival

NOW THAT THOSE DARK YEARS are over and I am free from the pain hurt, and shame, and as I look back, it all seems like it only happened over a matter of a few years. I totally agree with the Bible when it reads:

"… For what is your life? It is even a vapour, that appeareth for a little time, and then vanisheth away." (James 4:14 KJV)

It seems like it was not so long ago that all of these things happened to me. It is compared to the feeling after the birth of a child. During labor, the pain hurts beyond words, yet, when the child has delivered, and outside of the womb, the pains are just a memory. So are the years of suffering through the abuse. It all seems like a nightmare from which I have awakened; only it was not a nightmare, it was real.

There were many things that I learned as I traveled the journey of healing. But there are a few things that I hold very dear:

* Forgiveness is the most vital and compelling part of overcoming hurt and pain from any trauma

Sometimes, society does not like including God in some things; however, I believe that the Bible is the most positive and rewarding thing that exists. It holds principles that are natural **and** spiritual, and those principles do not change. It doesn't matter if one is a Christian or not, some principles apply to life across the board, and they are sound and unmovable. The principle of forgiveness is an existing law that holds true even if people do not believe it, embrace it, or exercise it. Forgiveness brings hope, light, and freedom, and it releases us from the prison of pain and hurt. But more than anything, God declares that He will not forgive us if we do not forgive one another:

"But if you forgive not men their trespasses, neither will your Father forgive your trespasses". (Matthew 6:15 KJV)

When we fail to forgive, we place ourselves above God. And it is a dangerous thing to put oneself above God. If God can forgive us for cursing Him, lying, deceiving, fornicating, stealing, murdering, cheating, and all other evils, (in which He does forgive us) surely, we can forgive one another. Failing to forgive those who hurt and harm us ties God's hands from forgiving us. All that we do or have done in the past against God is held against us until we forgive. If we hold unforgiveness in our hearts, we will not see God's face in peace because we have violated one of His principles which state:

"And when ye stand praying, forgive, if ye have ought against any: that your Father also which is in heaven may forgive you your trespasses." (Mark 11:25 KJV)

God did not say that forgiving others would be easy; however, I do not believe that He will tell us to do something that we cannot do. And He, Himself was our perfect example because He forgave us first and is always forgiving us. Peter asked Jesus a question:

[21] Then came Peter to him, and said, Lord, how oft shall my brother sin against me, and I forgive him? till seven times? [22] Jesus saith unto him, I say not unto thee, Until seven times: but, Until seventy times seven. (Matthew 18:21-22)

✻ Everything changes; nothing stays the same

79

When we fail to deal with our issues, push them farther and farther into the past, ignore them, or simply let them linger without giving them attention, believe me when I tell you, they will not just go away. It will stifle our lives. I am of the persuasion that when we have issues, and we fail to acknowledge and resolve them, as we grow, they grow. As we mature, the issues mature also.

We sometimes try to fool ourselves that if we ignore the problem, it will go away. However, this is an ostrich's perspective and does not pan out. The issue will follow us and as we learn and mature, so will the issue, until finally, we either die, or the issue catches up with us. It is easier to deal with the issue than to have the issue deal with us. When an issue deals with us, we are not the ones in control. However, when we take control of the issue and deal with it, we have the power of overcoming it. At some point, things will change.

* Life is too short to hold on to negative things of the past

We have only one life to live, and it is shorter for some than it is for others. Holding on to the past breeds misery when it is filled with hatred and un-forgiveness. When we do not let go, it gives the person or people who perpetrated the evil control of our future. Even though he is not alive, I had to forgive the relative who molested me when I was a child. I had to come to grips that it happened, that it hurt, I cannot go back and retrieve my virginity, or erase what happened. I had to let go of all elements that held me back from being liberated and happy. It was truly a process, but at some point, I had to say, enough! Establishing that enough was enough took me to the Cross, into the face of God, on the altar, and on my way to freedom.

During the process of deliverance, I spent lots of time in the bathtub, washing my body as I talked to God. My best and most productive prayer time was relaxing in the bathtub. For hours sometimes, I sat in the tub washing, singing, worshiping and praising God. Sometimes, I praised Him with tears rolling down my face and my heart heavy. Other times, I bathed and worshiped while thinking on how God's mercy and grace kept me; thanking and loving on Him for his love, patience, understanding, and compassion for me. I realized later that symbolically, I was washing away the shame, hurt, humiliation, guilt, and torment. I was also demonstratively washing away my mistakes and bad choices. It was a package deal for me. What a process, what an experience, and what a joy to be free!

❀ God never leaves or forsakes us

The last thing that I hold dear to my heart from the journey was that God is forever present in our lives, and opening up to Him opens the door to freedom. Although we want to be free of issues, the freedom that we desire doesn't come as easy as saying it. The hardest thing for me was to go to God with all that stuff. It took humility and sincerity. Freedom was waiting in the wings, but there was a process to freedom. Acknowledging that it happened, confessing my feelings and thoughts, and going over the things that happened to me were significant hurdles. Once I accomplished this stuff, then and only then I was I ready.

The beautiful thing about the entire journey is that God was always there. He was with me every step of the way. It is His good pleasure to deliver. He was waiting for me to come to Him; I was not waiting for Him to come to me. He knew from the very beginning that I needed Him and that I did not know what to do, where to go, or with whom to talk. I learned that I could come clean with God, not holding back anything. Whether we want to acknowledge it or not, we are naked before God. We have no privacy, and nothing belongs to us. We came here with nothing and will leave with nothing. So, why not come clean, open, raw, and naked before Him?

CHAPTER 20

Rape in the Bible

❧

CSA IS NOT A NEW issue. Rape, especially, goes back as far as the Old Testament. It is interesting to note that every time rape occurred, death and bloodshed followed. The first documented rape in the Bible happened with Jacob's daughter, Dinah. Shechem, son of Hamor, raped Dinah. Her brothers, Simeon and Levi, avenged her rape by leading an attack against the entire city of Shechem, murdering the rapist, his father, and all of the males of the clan. They confiscated their flock and all of their wealth and took their wives and children captive. They rescued Dinah, their sister out of the camp. (Genesis 34)

In the next documented case, a Levite's concubine was sexually assaulted all night long by a band of Benjamites. The Levite cut her body into twelve pieces and sent one piece to each tribe of Israel. The other tribes wanted the perpetrators to come forward so that the camp could be cleansed of the sin. But they did not come forward. After receiving the concubine's body parts, the other tribes avenged her death by going into war and killing all but 600 of 26,700 men of the tribe of Benjamin. An entire tribe was nearly annihilated because of the sexual assault of a concubine. (Judges 19-21)

The next recorded rape was King David's daughter, Tamar, who was sexually assaulted by her brother, Amnon. Absalom, Amnon, and Tamar were siblings. Absalom avenged Tamar's rape by having Amnon killed while he was drunk. (2 Samuel 13:8-29)

The last documented sexual assault was that aginst King David's concubines. Absalom, King David's son, sexually assaulted King David's concubines. He violated them at a place that all Israel could see because he was in a war with his father. I perceive that the act perpetrated against these concubines is an example that rape is not an act of a need for sex, but is an act of power and control. (2 Samuel 16:21-22)

Another interesting fact about rape in the Bible is that the rape of a virgin bound a man to marry her and be with her the rest of her life without putting her away. (Deuteronomy 22:28, 29)

CHAPTER 21

The Accountability Issue

❧

I FEEL THAT IN OUR country, the system does not take sexual abuse against children seriously enough. As a matter of fact, according to one statistic, [1]from 2005 to 2009, "Congress cut federal funding to states to treat and protect abused and neglected children by 17%." Men can molest, rape, and abuse men, women, and children and sometimes only receive sentences equal to a slap on the wrist. I wonder if the reason for such lenient sentences is because men predominately rule the criminal justice system. [2]According to the American Constitution Society, "the number of women judges, since 1998 has increased to 496 from 302, and in 2009, male judges exceeded 1,500. It further details that gender diversity is severely lacking."

When children are victims of sexual abuse, the majority of their lives may be spent trying to overcome the trauma, while a man can perpetrate it and receive sentences that are so short and meaningless that they are insulting, and show just how much this country cares about the children. There is a reason why every time rape occurred in the Bible someone or some people paid with their lives. Yes, God did approve of capital punishment in the Old Testament – not only for rape but also for incest (Leviticus 20).

CSA in America is widespread and crosses all religious, economic, social, and racial barriers. The effects of CSA have changed the course of our society and staggered the minds of the clergy, professionals, and clinicians all over the world. There is a remarkable increase in the prison population because of CSA.

We are all affected directly or indirectly by it. The spirit of it is evil, demonic, cruel, and is continuously and strategically perpetuated by the hordes of hell. CSA is an act of power and control and is perpetuated by individuals who feel they have no power or control over their lives, which is why they target certain people. Abusers target those that they believe are most vulnerable.

It is urgent that single women in today's society choose their lovers or spouses very carefully. Women should be cautious when choosing baby-sitters. Our daily newspapers are filled with sad and unbelievable horror stories about boyfriends who molest, rape, and murder their girlfriend's daughters and sons while the mother is either at work or some other place. The stories are numerous.

I read a very disturbing report that [3]children living with their mother and her boyfriend are about 11 times more likely to be abused sexually, physically, or emotionally than children living with their biological parents. The report also indicates that "Likewise, children living with their mother and her boyfriend are six times more likely to be neglected physically, emotionally, or educationally than children living with their married biological parents." The same article further indicates that "one of the most dangerous places for a child is a home that includes an unrelated boyfriend; especially when the friend is left alone to care for the child." Conclusively, the article indicates that "children living with their mother's boyfriends were more than 45 times more likely to be killed than children living with married parents." It seems apparent sometimes that a boyfriend may feel disconnected from his girlfriend's children as one of the reasons they are prone to sexually abuse her children (along with other sick and psychotic reasons). [4]One study revealed that men who are not biologically related to their partner's children may not feel a connection to them."

Some mothers who leave their young children with boyfriends use denial and defensiveness as two means of reasoning. [5]"Denial is a psychological defense mechanism that a person uses to screen out distressing realities and the painful feelings they cause." Some mothers feel the need to leave their young children with their boyfriends because there is no other babysitter to keep the kids while they go to work. Better yet, the boyfriends may volunteer to babysit because of their hidden motive to molest the children. One question that I find in the scenario of the working mother and the boyfriend who is left behind babysitting is "why isn't the boyfriend out working?" Whatever the situation, the children are in the hands of sexual abusers.

Sexual abuse can be a generational issue. In my family, there are four consecutive generations of sexual assault. The [6]Yale Law & Policy Review reveals a study which shows that most often mothers are the link to the cycle of generational incest and that treating them may help break the cycle. They further reported that treatment would help mothers who are in denial "learn how to avoid victimization as it will serve as a healthier role model for their daughters." It was my life-long goal to protect my children from sexual abusers, whether they were family members or strangers. I understood the consequences of leaving young children alone with adults. And from personal experience, it didn't matter if it was a family member, a stranger, or a Christian.

Children are not psychologically, emotionally, mentally, or physically equipped to cope with sexual stimulation of any kind. Their bodies, minds, souls, and spirits are not mature or equipped to take on such a challenge. Every entity that comprises a child is thrown completely off-balance when they are stimulated sexually at such a young age. The act is inconceivable.

One thing that is terribly devastating about CSA is the fact that children are taught to honor, respect, and obey parental authority, and to submit to authority figures, but children are abused sexually by the very people who claim to love and protect them. Fathers, mothers, other family members, priests, police officers, doctors, educators and many other authority figures have failed children in protecting them from sexual abuse.

When some sexually abused children grow up to be adults, they continue to live in the bondage of pain and fear the rest of their lives. They harbor guilt, shame, hopelessness, despair, anxiety, and other emotions that result in the abuse. Sometimes the victims, as adults, project either their anger or pain onto their children or other children.

It is of vital importance that parents educate their children on sexual abuse; teach them the difference between an evil touch and an authentic touch; cover them with the blood of Jesus, and pray for them that God will protect them everywhere they go. I feel that parents should pray and guard their children against the madness of perverts who appear to have only one goal in life, and that is to abuse sexually as many children as they can without being apprehended.

Over the years, I concluded that the men with whom I was involved had some of the same issues that I did and were victims of something also. They did not know how to conduct themselves as men because mostly women raised them, or, their fathers were not proper role models. They surely did not know how to be husbands or parents. Maybe they were hurting just as I was hurting. Sometimes people project pain onto other people because they are hurting. Pain is sometimes the only thing with which hurting people are comfortable or can relate. My heart goes out to the men that I met, and I sometimes wonder what became of them.

God blessed me to be raised by a Christian mother. She taught me what she knew and could only teach me what she knew. The one thing that she taught me which will last forever was to have faith in God. Had it not been for God, I know that I would have lost my mind, committed suicide, been murdered by violence, or turned to drugs or alcohol to relieve my pain.

My heart aches for sexually abused girls and boys. My prayer to God is that they are rescued, ministered to, counseled, healed and delivered before one more child or adult commits suicide, falls into a state of irreversible despair, turn to drugs or alcohol for relief, or reverse the victim role and become the perpetrator. My prayer for the perpetrator is that they will seek help for their issue. I pray that they will discover that there is indeed hope for their problem and turn to Jesus Christ, the One who can heal them.

CONCLUSION

IT HAS BEEN TWENTY YEARS, I am still going strong, and I do not have regrets about single life. It has been a long journey, but I made it. My children are adults, and I even have three beautiful grandchildren. I have been able to breathe and get a grip on my new life. My accomplishments since the last marriage include two Master Degrees and a Graduate Certificate, and I am working toward my Ph.D.

Memories do not haunt me anymore. The dreams and visions have all dissipated. It gives me great pleasure to share with others the way in which God brought me through every phase and kept me with a sound mind. More than anything, I am grateful to God for His love, goodness, mercy and grace. Pleasing Him is the pivot of my life. Serving Him gives me untold gratification. And if He chooses to allow me to remarry, I will be quite grateful, but I say as Paul does; "…I have learned, in whatsoever state I am, therewith to be content."

SURVIVAL OF THE INNER MAN
(IN POETIC VICTORY)

I am free today, and I don't have to hide-
The fear and torment that I held inside.
The terrible grief and horrific pain-
Kept my life on a chaotic plane.

When I was a child is when it all began-
It kept on happening over and over again.
My spirit, soul, and body could not rest-
From the constant pain of the rape and incest.

I tried to suppress the pain and fear,
But each time I found myself drowning in tears.
I hoped and prayed that my wound would heal;
I believed that my freedom was in God's will.

Sometimes I felt sad, depressed, and confused-
At times I felt lonely, degraded, and used;
The haunting dreams and perpetual grief-
Caused me to pant spasmodically for relief.

How could anyone have been so horribly vile-
As to take such advantage of an innocent child-
And put her to silence, via stripping her soul-
And violating her right to be vital and whole;

By robbing her of her power of choice-
And ignoring the plea of her tacit voice;
Taking her innocence, which she cannot reclaim-
Leaving her to suffer the horror and shame.

But vengeance was sure; it is Biblically sound,
Justice was certain and did come around;
Restoration was inevitable; it happened at last-
Ultimately, that nightmare is now in the past.
This poem was written after I left the city of Chicago and
rededicated my life to Christ.

GOD BROUGHT ME BACK

So, you're back out there in the world of sin,
Your life is worse now than it's ever been;
You're running over here and running over there-
But unable to find peace anywhere.

Deep down in your heart, you want to be true,
But coming back to God seems so hard to do.
You go to the church, and you hear God's Word,
You're tempted to repent but don't have the nerves.

You say to yourself, "I want to do right,
But maybe I'll wait til tomorrow night."
Satan is glad you didn't listen to Christ,
Thinking he has a chance to take your life.

The Word of God is sticking with you this time-
As a backslider, you cannot get it out of your mind;
You know that the Lord is soon to come,
And you know when He does there'll be no place to run.

The Lord blesses you to see the next day.
His love and His mercy have led the way.
The Word of God is going forth again,
The Lord is warning you to repent of your sins.

Your heart is touched, and your mind is stirred,
But you can't seem to find the strength anywhere-
To lift up your feet and take the first step-
On your way to the altar to get God's help.

You've made up your mind that you want to be saved-
You no longer want to be one of satan's slaves;
God already knew what was in your heart-
He was waiting for you to make a start.

The minister is saying, "Please come to Christ,"
As if he's talking directly to you, and he knows your life.
Now is your chance live again-
To come out of hell, misery, and sin.

The Spirit and the flesh began to battle,
But your heart is fixed, and your mind is settled;
You start to feel light and warm inside-
Cause the Lord has strengthened you to walk down that aisle.

Oh, what joy that fills your soul!
The Lord, Jesus Christ is making you whole;
You begin to think of how good God is-
Then your eyes start to be filled with tears;

First, tears of how sorry you are for your sins,
And that you will never turn your back on God again;
Then comes the tears of gladness and joy-
Like a little baby child with her very first toy.

The Spirit of God has taken control,
You feel deliverance deep down in your soul;
You're thanking the Lord for all He has done-
And how you know that He'll never leave you alone.

Thank God, Almighty, my soul is saved,
From misery, torment, hell, and the grave;
Thank God, Almighty for His love for me-
That saved my soul and set me free.

CHAPTER 2

The In-Between Years

1. www.mayoclinic.org/diseases-conditions/dissociative-disorders/.../con-20031012

CHAPTER 3

The Dark Years/The Lost Girl

1. "Filicide." *Wikipedia.* Wikimedia Foundation, Web. 16 Aug. 2016.

2. Draper, E. (2011, May 26). Parents who kill their kids not always insane, expert says. *The Denver Post.* Retrieved August 16, 2016, from http://www.denverpost.com/2011/05/26/parents-who-kill-their-kids-not-always-insane-expert-says/

3. http://www.childabusestories.org/factss/15510-children-died-child-abuse-and-neglect-during-2001-2010-period

CHAPTER 5

Imprint on the Soul

1. Bowater, Margaret. "Redeeming the fruit fly: Redecision work with a recurring dream." *Transactional Analysis Journal* 40.2 (2010): 95-98.

2. Morgan, A. (2014, January 10). Recurring Dreams: Your Dreams Are Trying to Tell You Something! Huffington Post. Retrieved January 20, 2017

3. Carr, M. (2014, November 13). What's Behind Your Recurring Dreams? Retrieved May, 2016, from https://www.psychologytoday.com/blog/dream-factory/201411/whats-behind-your-recurring-dreams

4. Floyd, K. (2013, August). What Lack of Affection Can Do to You. Retrieved May 17, 2016, from https://www.psychologytoday.com/blog/affectionado/201308/what-lack-affection-can-do-you

CHAPTER 11
Understanding Child Sexual Abuse

1. Andrews, G., Corry, J., Slade, T., Issakidis, C., & Swanston, H. (2004). Child sexual abuse. *Comparative quantification of health risks: global and regional burden of disease attributable to selected major risk factors*, 2, 1851-940.

2. Child Sexual Abuse: What Parents Should Know," American Psychological Association. (http://www.apa.org/pi/families/resources/child-sexual-abuse.aspx) (February 19, 2014)

3. Arata, C. (2002) Child Sexual Abuse and Sexual Revictimization. *Clinical Psychology*, 9: 135-164.

4. Wolak, J., Mitchell, K. J., & Finkelhor, D. (2006). *Online Victimization of Youth: Five Years Later.*

5. Child Maltreatment 2012," U.S. Department of Health and Human Services, Administration for Children and Families, Administration on Children, Youth and Families, Children's Bureau.

6. Facts about Sexual Assault. Retrieved May 24, 2016, from https://cmsac.org/facts-and-statistics/

7. Miller, K. L., Dove, M. K., & Miller, S. M. (2007, October). *A counselor's guide to child sexual abuse: Prevention, reporting and treatment strategies.* Paper based on a program presented at the Association for Counselor Education and Supervision Conference, Columbus, OH.

8. Hegazy, A. A., & Al-Rukban, M. O. (2012). *The Health.* Hymen: facts and conceptions, 3, 109-115.

9. Cook, R., & Dickens, B. (2009). Hymen reconstruction: Ethical and legal issues. *International Journal of Gynecology Obstetrics*, 107(3), 266-269.

10. Rich, P. (2005). Understanding and Treating Sexually Abusive Behavior in Children and Adolescents. In New York State Association for the Treatment of Sexual Abusers and New York State Alliance of Sex Offender Service Providers (p. 16). New York, NY: Stetson School. Retrieved from http://www.nysatsa.com/conference/2010Workshops/Rich%20 Handout%20NYATSA%20Understanding%20and%20Treating%20 SAB%20Children-Adolescents.pdf

11. Day, A., Thurlow, K., & Woolliscroft, J. (2003). Working with childhood sexual abuse: A survey of mental health professionals. Child Abuse and Neglect, 27, 191-198. Retrieved January 18, 2017.

12. http://cmhadurham.ca/mental-health/dissociative-identity-disorder-did/

13. Ross, C. A. (1989). Multiple personality disorder: Diagnosis, clinical features, and treatment. John Wiley & Sons.

14. Paolucci, E., Genuis, M., & Violato, C. (2001). A meta-analysis of the published research on the effects of child sexual abuse [Abstract]. *Journal of Psychology, 135*(1), 17-36

15. Maniglio, R. (2009). The Impact of Child Sexual Abuse on Health: A systematic review of reviews. *Clinical Psychology Review, 29 (7)*, 647-57.

16. Maltz, R. (2002). Treating the Sexual Intimacy Concerns of Sexual Abuse Survivors. *Sexual Relationship Therapy, 17*(4), 321-327.

17. Putnam, F. (2003). Ten-year research update review: Child sexual [Abstract]. *Journal of American Academy of Child & Adolescent Psychiatry, 42*(3), 269-278.

18. Kendler, K. (2000). Childhood sexual abuse and adult psychiatric and substance use disorders in women: An epidemiological and co-twin control analysis. [Abstract]. *Archives of General Psychiatry, 57*(10), 983-959.

19. Simpson, T., & Miller, W. (2002). Concomitance between child-hood sexual and physical abuse and substance use problems: A review. *Clinical Psychology Review, 22*(1) 27-77. Retrieved May 18, 2016, from sciencedirect.com/science/article/pii/S027273580000088X.

20. http://www.ncsl.org/research/human-services/homeless-and-run-away-youth.aspx.

21. Menzel, M. (2013, August 23). Runaway teens at risk to become human trafficking victims, Florida experts say. Naples Daily News.

22. Riley, B., Greif. G. L., Caplan, D. L., & Macaulay, H. K. *American Journal of Family Therapy*, 32, 139-153. Retrieved January 18, 2017.

23. Thrane, L. E., Hoyt, D. R., Whitbeck, L. B., & Yoder, K. A. (2006). Impact of family abuse on running away, deviance, and street victimization

among homeless rural and urban youth. Child abuse & neglect, 30(10), 1117-1128.

24. Day, A., Thurlow, K., & Woolliscroft, J. (2003). Working with childhood sexual abuse: A survey of mental health professionals. Child Abuse & Neglect, (27), 191-198.

25. Noll, J. T. (2003). A Prospective Investigation on the impact of childhood sexual abuse on the development of sexuality. Journal of Consulting and Clinical Psychology, 71, 575-586.

26. U.S. Census Bureau, Statistical Abstract of the United States: 2011: Available at: http://www.census.gov/compendia/statab/2011/tables/11s 1336.pdf

27. Long, L., Burnett, J., & Thomas, R. (2006). Sexuality Counseling: An Integrative Approach. Upper Saddle River, NJ: Pearson.

28. Ratican, K. (1992). Sexual abuse survivors: Identifying symptoms and special treatment considerations. Journal of Counseling and Development, 71(1), 33-38.

29. Gil, E. (1991). The Healing Power of Play: Working with Abused Children. New, NY: Guilford Press.

30. Rohde, P., Simon, G. E., Ludman, E. J., Linde, J. A., Jeffery, R. W., & Operskalski, B. H. (2008). Associations of child sexual and physical abuse with obesity and depression in middle-aged women. *Child Abuse & Neglect*, 32, 878-887. Retrieved January 18, 2017.

31. U.S. Census Bureau, Statistical Abstract of the United States: 2011: Available at: http://www.census.gov/compendia/statab/2011/tables/11s 1336.pdf

CHAPTER 12
The Male and Child Sexual Abuse

1. Rotheram-Borus, M. J., Mahler, K. H., & Koopman, C. (1996). Sexual Abuse History and Associated Multiple Risk Behavior in Runaways [Abstract]. *American Journal of Orthopsychiatry, 66*(3), 390-400.

2. Dorahy, M., & Clearwater, K. (2012). Shame and Guilt in men exposed to childhood sexual abuse: A qualitative investigation. *Journal of Child Sexual Abuse, 2*(12), 155-175.

3. Hunter, S. V. Disclosure of Child Sexual Abuse as a Life-long Process: Implications for Health Professionals. *The Australian and New Zealand Journal of Family Therapy, 32*.2 (2011): 159-72. Web

4. O'Leary, P. J., and J. Barber. Gender Differences in Silencing following Childhood Sexual Abuse. *Journal of Child Sexual Abuse* 17.2 (2008): 133-43. Web.

5. McBride, K. (Ed.). (2011, March 25). Child Sexual Abuse and Narcissism: Blaming the victim expands the trauma. *Psychology Today.* doi:https://www.psychologytoday.com/blog/the-legacy-distorted-love/201103/child-sexual-abuse-and-narcissism

6. Facts About Sexual Assault. Retrieved May 24, 2016, from https://cmsac.org/facts-and-statistics/

7. Dykman, R. A., McPherson, B., Ackerman, P. T., Newton, J. E., Mooney, D. M., Wherry, J., & Chaffin, M. (1997). Internalizing and externalizing characteristics of sexually and/or physically abused children. *Integrative Physiological and Behavioral Science, 32*(1), 62-83

8. Garnefski, N., & Diekstra, R. F. (1997). Child sexual abuse and emotional and behavioral problems in adolescence: Gender differences.

Journal of the American Academy of Child & Adolescent Psychiatry, *36*(3), 323-329.

9. *When Males Have Been Sexually Abused as Children: A Guide for Men*. (2015, April 14). Retrieved May 26, 2016, from http://www.phac-aspc. gc.ca/sfv-avf/sources/nfnts/nfnts-visac-male/index-eng.php

10. Steever, E. E., Follette, V. M., & Naugle, A. E. (2001). The correlates of male adults' perceptions of their early sexual experiences. *Journal of Traumatic Stress, 14*(1), 189-205.\

11. Roberts, R., O'Connor, T., Dunn, J., & Golding, J. (2004). The effects of child sexual abuse in later family life, mental health, parenting and adjustment of offspring. *Child Abuse and Neglect, 28*(5), 525-545.

12. Sedlak, A. J., Mettenburg, J., Basena, M., Petta, I., McPherson, K., Greene, A., & Li, S. (2010). Fourth National Incidence Study of Child Abuse and Neglect (NIS–4): Report to Congress, Executive Summary. (Rep.). Retrieved January 19, 2017.

CHAPTER 13
Child Sexual Abuse from a Spiritual Perspective

1. *Pigs in the Parlor: A Practical Guide to Deliverance*. (1973). Kirkwood, MO: Impact Books.

2. *Amplified Bible*. (2015). LaHabra, CA: The Lockman Foundation.

CHAPTER 14
Child Sexual Abuse from a Clinic/Psychological Perspective

1. http://www.benbenjamin.net/pdfs/Issue2.pdf

2. https://en.wikipedia.org/wiki/**Sublimation_(psychology)**

3. Wakefield, H. (2006). The Effects of Child Sexual Abuse: Truth Versus Political Correctness. *Issues in Child Abuse Accusations, 16*(1), 2.

4. McCloskey, L., & Walker, M. (2000). Posttraumatic stress in children exposed to family violence and single-event trauma. *Diagnostic and Statistical Manual of Mental Disorders, 39*, 105-115.

5. http://www.childluresprevention.com/research/report.asp

CHAPTER 15
Soul Murder

1. Vachss, A. (1994, August 1). You Can Carry the Cure in Your Own Heart. *Parade.*

2. Hutchison, L., & Mueller, D. (2008). Sticks and Stones and Broken Bones. *Sticks and Stones and Broken Bones: The Influence of Parental Verbal Abuse on Peer Related Victimization, 9*(1), 17-30.

CHAPTER 16
Disconnecting the Music from the Soul

1. Jancke, L. (August 8, 2008). Music, memory and emotion. *Journal of Biology, 7*(6), 21. Retrieved June 3, 2016.

2. https://en.wikipedia.org/wiki/Autobiographical_memory

3. Salimpoor, V., Benevoy, M., Larcher, K., Dagher, A., & Zatorre, R. (2011). Anatomically distinct dopamine release during anticipation and experience of peak emotion to music. *Nature Neuroscience, 14,*

257-262. Retrieved June 3, from http://www.nature.com/neuro/journal/v14/n2/abs/nn.2726.html

CHAPTER 21
The Accountability Issue

1. http://www.childabusestories.org/factss/15510-children-died-child-abuse-and-neglect-during-2001-2010-period

2. Sugameli, G. (2010, November 30). Male Judges Far Outnumber Women Judges, Federal Court Graph Shows. Retrieved August 31, 2016, from http://www.acslaw.org/acsblog/male-judges-far-out-number-women-judges-federal-court-graph-shows.

3. Wilcox, B. (2011, April 22). Suffer the Little Children: Cohabitation and the Abuse of America's Children. Retrieved June 3, from www.thepublicdiscourse.com/2011/04/3181/

4. Berger, L. M., Paxson, C., & Waldfogel, J. (2009). Mothers, Men, and child protective services involvement. *Child Maltreatment*, 14(3), 263-276.

5. Thomas, C. L. (1998). Taber's Cyclopedic Medical Dictionary (16th ed.). Philadelphia, PA: F. A. Davis Company.

6. Adams, Christine (1994) "Mothers Who Fail to Protect Their Children from Sexual Abuse: Addressing the Problem of Denial," Yale Law & Policy Review: Vol. 12: Iss. 2, Article 7.
Available at: http://digitalcommons.law.yale.edu/ylpr/vol12/iss2/7